Hanoi Tourism, Vietnam
Travel Guide, History Information

Author
David Mills.

SONITTEC PUBLISHING. All rights reserved. No part of this publication may be reproduced, distributed, or transmitted in any form or by any means, including photocopying, recording, or other electronic or mechanical methods, without the prior written permission of the publisher, except in the case of brief quotations embodied in critical reviews and certain other noncommercial uses permitted by copyright law. For permission requests, write to the publisher, addressed "Attention: Permissions Coordinator," at the address below.

Copyright © 2019 Sonittec Publishing
All Rights Reserved

First Printed: 2019.

Publisher:
SONITTEC LTD
College House, 2nd Floor
17 King Edwards Road,
Ruislip
London
HA4 7AE.

Table of Content

SUMMARY	1
INTRODUCTION	3
HISTORY	7
MODERN HISTORY	7
RECENT HISTORY	10
PRE 20TH CENTURY HISTORY	10
GEOGRAPHY AND CLIMATE	12
ADMINISTRATIVE ZONES	13
HANOI'S PEOPLE	14
SPECIAL FEATURES IN HANOI	16
Hanoi 36 streets	16
Some streets in Old Quarter	21
TOURISM	30
SAFETY IN HANOI	30
Avoiding scams in Hanoi	33
Avoiding taxi scams in Hanoi	36
TRANSPORTATION	40
Getting from the airport into Hanoi	40
Getting around	54
ATTRACTIONS	57
Temples	57
Hoe Nhai Pagoda	57
One Pillar Pagoda	57
Ngoc Son Temple	58
Temple of Literature	60
Tran Quoc Pagoda	61
Pho Linh Tay Ho Pagoda	63
Tay Ho Temple	65
Bach Ma Temple	67
Ba Da Pagoda	68
Museums	69
Hanoi Police Museum	69
Ho Chi Minh Museum	70
Vietnam Military History Museum	72
Hoa Lo Prison (Hanoi Hilton)	73
Vietnamese Women's Museum	74
Vietnam Museum of Ethnology	76
National Museum of Vietnamese History	78
Vietnam Fine Arts Museum	80
The Ho Chi Minh Trail Museum	81

Public parks and zoos 84
    Hoan Kiem Lake 84
    Thong Nhat Park 85
    West Lake 87
Art galleries or venues 88
    Mosaic wall 88
    Art galleries 90
Markets 91
    Quang Ba Flower Market 91
    Chau Long Market 93
    Long Bien Market 94
    Dong Xuan market 96
General activities 98
    Gyms 98
    Lacquerware classes 101
    What to do with kids in Hanoi 102
    Lotus flowers 103
Churches 105
    Cua Bac 105
    St Joseph's Cathedral 106
Hiking, walking tours and itineraries 108
    One day in Hanoi 108
    Two days on a budget in Hanoi 112
    Four days in Hanoi 114
    Hanoi on a splurge 116
    Which is the best street food tour in Hanoi? 118
Shopping 123
    Shopping in Hanoi 123
    Hanoi's 36 streets 124
    Buying a secondhand motorbike 125
Day trips 127
    Perfume Pagoda 127
    Booking a Ha Long Bay cruise 129
    Two or three days in Ha Long Bay? 132
    Hanoi to Mai Chau by motorbike 134
    Bat Trang ceramic village 137
    An overnight trip to Tam Dao 138
    Cu Da, or Vermicelli Village 142
    Motorbike trips 146
    Dau pagoda and Horn village 148
    Bang So (Bamboo village) 150
    Exploring Bac Kan province 153
    Thay and Tay Phuong Pagodas 155
    Co Loa Citadel 158

- Ba Vi National Park 159
- Performing arts 163
  - Thang Long Water Puppets 163
- Massages and spas 164
  - Where can I get a good massage in Hanoi? 164
- Giving back 166
  - Humanitarian Services for Children of Vietnam 166
- Interesting buildings 169
  - Heritage house at 87 Ma May St 169
  - Hanoi Opera House 170
- Historic attractions 171
  - Ho Chi Minh's Mausoleum 171
  - Presidential Palace and Ho Chi Minh's House on Stilts 172
  - Chuong Duong Bridge 173
  - Thang Long Citadel 174
  - Long Bien Bridge 176

FRONT GUIDE 177
- Surviving Hanoi traffic on foot 177
- The Essentials 179
- Spending in Hanoi? 191
- Getting a local SIM card in Hanoi 194
- Weather & climate 195
- When's the best time to visit Hanoi? 198

Summary

The world is a book and those who do not travel read only one page.

It is indeed very unfortunate that some people feel traveling is a sheer waste of time, energy and money. Some also find traveling an extremely boring activity. Nevertheless, a good majority of people across the world prefer traveling, rather than staying inside the confined spaces of their homes. They love to explore new places, meet new people, and see things that they would not find in their homelands. It is this very popular attitude that has made tourism, one of the most profitable, commercial sectors in the world.

People travel for various reasons. Some travel for work, others for fun, and some for finding mental peace. Though every person may have his/her own reason to go on a journey, it is essential to note that traveling, in itself, has some inherent advantages. For one, for some days getting away from everyday routine is a pleasant change. It not only refreshes one's body, but also mind and soul. Traveling to a distant place and doing exciting things that are not thought of otherwise, can rejuvenate a person, who then returns home, ready to take on new and more difficult challenges in life and work. It makes a person forget his worries, problems, frustrations, and fears, albeit for some time. It gives him a chance to think wisely and constructively. Traveling also helps to heal; it can mend a broken heart.

For many people, traveling is a way to attain knowledge, and perhaps, a quest to find answers to their questions. For this, many people prefer to go to faraway and isolated places. For believers, it is a search for God and to gain higher knowledge; for others, it is a search for inner peace. They might or might not find what they are looking for, but such an experience certainly enriches their lives

Introduction

(Cinet)- Ha Noi, the capital of Socialist Republic of Vietnam, is the political - economic - cultural - scientific and technological center of the whole country. Ha Noi ranks second and first in terms of population and area respectively. It is in the list of 17 cities with the largest area in the world.

Ha Noi borders Thai Nguyen, Vinh Phuc provincies in the North, Ha Nam, Hoa Binh provincies in the South, Bac Giang, Bac Ninh and Hung Yen provincies in the East. The province covers an area of 3.324,92 square kilometres, and its population was 6.448.837 peoples (according to statistic in 2009).

Cultural Resources

Cultural Heritage

Hanoi has the most relics in the country including 1,952 relics in old Hanoi, 3053 historical monuments in Ha Tay, 170 monuments in Me Linh district and 4 communes of Luong Son district (Hoa Binh).

The number of relics ranked accounts for 42.65% (2,209 monuments) including two world cultural heritage: the central sector of Imperial citadel of Thang Long Ha Noi, the temple of LiteratureImperial Academy (Quoc Tu Giam) with 82 stone steles honouring doctoral candidates in Le Mac Dynasty (Documentary heritage from World Memorial program).

Hanoi, one of the most beautiful of the colonial Indochinese cities, is often the start or end point of a trip to Vietnam, and what a great welcome or farewell it is. Oozing with charm, Hanoi has gone through wholesale changes since Vietnam swung open its doors to tourism, but it remains true to its essential personality and is an amazing city to experience.

Though considerably quieter than big sister Saigon, Hanoi still retains a vibrant atmosphere. From the early hours until late at night, the fig-tree shaded streets swarm with careening motorbikes, often with four, five or even six people aboard. A cyclo is available on most street corners, but unless you are making a particularly long trip, the best way to explore Hanoi is by foot.

It seems that in Hanoi, no two streets meet at 90 degrees and there so many one-way thoroughfares it sometimes feels like you can't get there from here, nor here from there. Count on getting lost. But a day of dodging traffic and elbowing your way through overcrowded footpaths is exactly how most people spend their time in Hanoi, and it's more fun than any purpose-built tourist attraction. Keep a map close at hand though, so when you find something that tickles your fancy, you can mark it down otherwise you risk never finding it again.

Hanoi has a number of lovely parks and museums where you can while away the hours of a warm summer's afternoon Lenin Park, south of Hoan Kiem district and just north of Bay Kau Lake are among the most popular, especially on holidays, when it's packed with picnickers.

In winter months, you can find yourself a cozy cafe to snuggle up in, or find a streetside restaurant boiling up a pot of something belly-warming and delicious. While Hanoians are certainly happy to be free of the French occupation, they continue to embrace French culinary culture

Big, fat, fresh baguettes are sold everywhere, good for a pate sandwich or smeared with the ubiquitous Laughing Cow cheese. The coffee is world class served strong and rich in demitasses with the best blends being smooth and chocolatey. Wine is widely available, though inadequate storage and rotation lead to some bad bottles.

Specialty places like The Warehouse on Hang Trong are good for a wide, reliable selection of domestic and foreign vintages. And, of course, the pasteries beckon too. Hanoi has a plentiful and delicious collection of patisseries spread all over the city boasting decadent but very affordable treats.

Finally, the people of Hanoi are some of the warmest and most approachable in the country. Though English is not as commonly spoken as in the South, many of the older generation have a working vocabulary of French. Regardless of language, people will attempt to have a conversation with you irrespective of whether you can understand them. Many of the city's cyclo drivers speak some English and often have intriguing pasts that they are now willing to discuss with foreigners.

In Hanoi, you may find yourself sitting in a cafe sipping excellent coffee, nibbling a pastry, chatting in French to an old gentleman sporting a beret, while looking out on a vista of French-style buildings in the shadows of fig trees. You may begin to doubt that you got off the plane in the right city. But then, sitting at a streetside restaurant, slurping up a bowl of *bun cha* with a side of fresh springrolls, watching the 'yoke ladies' trundle by in their conical hats, hawking their wares nope, it's not Paris warmed over ... It's full-on Hanoi, a city to be savoured.

History

Modern History

As it had under Chinese rule, Vietnamese nationalism simmered quietly throughout the country, waiting for an opportunity. Young Nguyen Tat Thanh, better known by his alias Ho Chi Minh, thought that the end of WWI was a good opening, so he tried to present a plan for an independent Vietnam to US president Woodrow Wilson at the 1919 Versailles Peace Conference. Evidently, self-determination was for Europeans alone. When France fell to Nazi Germany in 1940, the Vichy government allowed the Japanese to put troops in Vietnam. The United States knew enough not to count on any French resistance, instead opting to pump arms and funding into the communist-dominated Viet Minh forces. Our leader, Ho Chi Minh, graciously accepted and began harassing the Japanese mercilessly.

After the bombing of Hiroshima and Nagasaki, Uncle Ho called for a general uprising known as the August Revolution, and on September 2, 1945, Ho Chi Minh and his National Liberation Committee (with US officials at his side) declared the Democratic Republic of Vietnam independent at a rally in Ba Dinh Square. The French were not pleased, and fought the Viet Minh tooth and nail for eight years, despite a massive military aid package from the USA and formal recognition by both China and the USSR. On May 7, 1954, the French threw in the towel and surrendered North Vietnam to the Viet Minh. Fiercely anti-communist leader Ngo Dinh Diem was elected (more or less; a lot of dead people voted in that election) president of South Vietnam. Soon afterward, the USA closed its consulate in Hanoi. In 1959, Southern cadres asked that the North Vietnamese join them in 'armed struggle' against the Diem regime. Hanoi responded by agreeing to help the National Liberation Front (NLF), also known as the Viet Cong, who were mainly communist South Vietnamese resisters with little training. Without French troops, however, the South Vietnamese army was incredibly weak, and the Western world looked on nervously as Diem began losing control of the situation.

The USA sent 2000 'military advisers' to South Vietnam in 1961, the number swelling to 23,000 by 1964. By then, Hanoi was no longer helping the NLF out with guns and training; they were sending trained North Vietnamese troops across the border. Despite small victories, Hanoi's war didn't seem winnable until the 1968 Tet Offensive, when Hanoi gained the upper hand. The USA continued to throw warm bodies to the tune of 3.14 million men and women at the increasingly bloody conflict until the 1973 cease-fire. The USA evacuated almost all troops out of Vietnam in return for Hanoi's commitment to keep communism above the 17th parallel. They also cut off most financial and other aid to South Vietnam. By 1975, the southern half of the country was running on fumes. North Vietnam launched a massive attack on the South on January 1975; Saigon surrendered in April. No one, least of all the leadership in Hanoi, was prepared for reunification. At least two million Vietnamese had died in the conflict and scars ran deep; the environment and economy were shambles. The violence wasn't over, either: In 1979, answering for Vietnam's 1978 invasion of Cambodia, China attacked Hanoi. The Chinese were repelled within 17 brutal days. The 1980s witnessed a devastating famine that left Hanoi with rice shortages and strict rations, a continuing guerrilla war with the Khmer Rouge in Cambodia and the opening of European communism. Surprisingly, Vietnam finished the decade in much better shape than it started. In February 1990, the government called for more 'openness and criticism', but was unprepared for the seething discontent behind the floodgates. Hanoi backtracked, but began allowing more economic openness while keeping government structure (and media access) in a lockbox. In 1992 Vietnam signed a peace treaty with Cambodia, and in 1994, the USA lifted economic sanctions on the country. The two former enemies now maintain diplomatic relations.

Recent History

As the economy continues to open to foreign investment and private ownership, Hanoi's leadership remains in the hands of hard-line communists. The economy's command structure insulated Vietnam from the worst of the Asian economic crisis (though its currency was devalued twice); the crisis actually increased confidence in the Communist Party. The growing private business sector in the city makes it obvious; however, that capitalism is making sturdy inroads into Vietnam. While the government is eyeing Most Favored Nation status with the US and, eventually, membership of the WTO, its human rights record is bound to be a stumbling block.

Pre 20th Century History

Human habitation of Northern Vietnam goes back about 500,000 years according to archaeological evidence. The site of present-day Hanoi has been populated for at least 10,000 years. These first inhabitants formed a feudally organized society that first relied on hunting, fishing and gathering, later developing animal husbandry and agriculture. These tribes developed in relative isolation until about 2000 years ago. The Han Chinese set up a military garrison near present-day Hanoi in 214 BC, using it as a base of operations that would eventually control most of modern Vietnam. The next 1000 years of Chinese rule introduced important technological innovations to the Vietnamese, including ploughs and irrigation systems. But rebellion simmered in every town, and the millennium was punctuated by revolution and resistance. This tradition of rebellion shaped Vietnam's national character.

Vietnamese rebels saw their chance when China's Tang dynasty collapsed. In 938, revolutionary leader Ngo Quyen gave the Chinese a sound whipping and established an independent Vietnamese state, but after his death the region fell into anarchy. In 980, Vietnam became a semi-independent client state of China, stabilizing the situation all for the cost of a biannual tribute. For the next 400 years, the site of present-day Hanoi served as the administrative seat for all of Vietnam. The Grand Royal enclosure, now the city's Old Quarter, was constructed and the nation's first university, the Temple of Literature, was founded during the first century of home rule. Attacks by the Khmers, Chinese and even Kublai Khan were repelled by national forces. All this was done with little Chinese interference. The Chinese never forgot their plum province, however, and in 1400 they captured Hanoi again. National hero Le Loi's guerrilla tactics and peasant support eventually reclaimed Vietnamese independence. A period of nationalism and renewed interest in Confucianism followed a reaction to increased discontent with Europeans, their values and their missionaries. The missionaries didn't take the hint, however, and in 1858 several were killed. The French had an excuse to invade, and by 1867 South Vietnam was a French colony. Hanoi was captured in 1874. The impotent imperial court was allowed to remain, indulging itself in various coups and capers, but the French controlled the nation.

Geography and climate

Hanoi is the capital city of Vietnam. It is located at 20°25' latitude North and 105°30' longitude East in the plains of North Vietnam. There are many rivers flowing eastwards to the sea. This is a convenient transport cluster for all the Northern provinces. The climate is tropical and affected by monsoons. There are four seasons in Hanoi, there are: Spring; it starts from February to April; average temperature is from 15° to 20°C (59° - 68° F), drizzle is frequent with wet weather. This is the season of the Lunar New Year holiday and many folk festivals. Summer; it starts from May to August; average temperature is from 30° to 36° C (86° - 97° F). There is much rain and sunshine. Autumn; it starts from September to November; average temperature is 25° to 36° C (75° 97°F). It is cool, clear and dry. This is the best season in Hanoi, but it is short, lasting no more than 50-60 days. Winter; it starts from December to January; the lowest temperature is from 10° to 15°C (48° -59 °F). The weather is cloudy and wet. The monsoons cause many phases of cold. The annual average rainfall in Hanoi is 1800 mm.

In the past, many rivers flowed through Hanoi, but they changed their currents from time to time, therefore the ground is mainly deposited by alluvium and there are many lakes. These rivers and lakes give Hanoi a natural beauty. In the flood season, the water level of the largest rivers flowing through Hanoi (the Red River, the Duong, Nhue, Day Rivers) rises very high. During ancient times, the Vietnamese people have built thousands of kilometers of dykes by the river banks. Nowadays, in the city, some sections of the ancient dykes have become traffic roads

Administrative zones

At the present time, Hanoi comprises 7 inner districts and 5 suburban districts. Nevertheless, districts may be increased in number as the capital is developing fast together with the country. The 7 inner districts of Hanoi are: Hoan Kiem district: This is a trade, cultural and administrative centre. The Municipal People's Committee, the Central Bank and important state offices are located in this district. It also includes theatres, railway stations, markets and busy commercial streets. There are two bridges link Hoan Kiem district with the other side of the Red River. Hoan Kiem Lake in the centre of the district is considered as the heart of the capital. Its ancient streets still keep deep imprints of Hanoi's millenary history; therefore they should be protected as historical relics. The Hoan Kiem lake description will be explain further in next chapter. Ba Dinh district: Ba Dinh district is located at South of West Lake, a zone where many highest state bodies and diplomatic offices are located. The Mausoleum and Museum of Ho Chi Minh and the Hanoi old citadel are also located in this district. The Western part of this district is being reconstructed through large projects. Hai Ba Trung district is situated of Hoan Kiem Lake including trade and administrative zones. It is developing southwards, covering some industrial and population localities between the National Road 1 A and the Red river. Dong Da district. This is a Southwest expanded part of the city including many common living quarters, colleges, hospitals and factories built in the 1960s and 1970s. Large transport routes and multi-storey buildings are now under construction in this district in the Southern part of Dong Da lake. Recently, the districts of Tay Ho, Thanh Xuan and Cau Giay have been formed on the territory of the old districts and precincts to satisfy the development demands of the city. In these new districts, the construction tempo has increased on the basis of the better planning. The suburban districts of Tu Liem and Thanh Tri are located in the South of the city; Dong Anh and Soc Son districts are in the North; and Gia Lam districts are in the East. Formerly, these districts were agricultural areas, providing the capital with food and vegetables. At present, new factories, industrial and export processing zones are being established in this district.

Hanoi's people

There was a long period in the northern part of the country of relative isolation from the west. Thus Vietnamese in Hanoi and its surrounding areas tend to be quite curious about westerners. Travelers should expect to be watched and commented on, and to be asked questions considered somewhat intrusive by western standards (how old are you, are you married, how much money do you make, why do you have those children, etc.). None of this is meant to cause offense; it is just a simple curiosity. Vietnamese live much more "out" in their neighborhoods than do typical westerners, who live and work in closed-up buildings and travel everywhere by car, and are avid observers of (and commentators on) life around them.

Hanoians are overwhelmingly honest and good-natured people. There is no animosity toward Americans left over from the war. People tend to be forward-looking and prefer not to dwell on the past; they are pragmatic, down-to-earth, and extremely hard-working, particularly women. Adults almost universally dote on children. Travelers can expect to have their babies taken away to be held, and their children of all ages entertained in shops, restaurants, and hotels.

Merchants and peddlers do see western travelers as great sources of income and relatively easy marks. They bargain aggressively and overcharge without mercy (but will scrupulously count change when the bargain is struck). Small children selling postcards and shoe shining services can be quite ruthless. People asking for hand-outs are very persistent and at times unpleasant. Travelers who walk purposefully, say "no" firmly to unwanted offers, and make minimal eye contact are fare best.

Special features in Hanoi

Hanoi 36 streets

History of Hanoi's Old quarter

As the oldest continuously developed area of Vietnam, Hanoi's Old Quarter has a history that spans 2,000 years and represents the eternal soul of the city. Located between the Lake of the Restored Sword, the Long Bien Bridge, a former city rampart, and a citadel wall, the Old Quarter started as a snake and alligator-infested swamp. It later evolved into a cluster of villages made up of houses on stilts, and was unified by Chinese administrators who built ramparts around their headquarters. The area was named "Dominated Annam" or "Protected South" by the Chinese.

The Old Quarter began to acquire its reputation as a crafts area when the Vietnamese attained independence in the 11th century and King Ly Thai to built his palace there. In the early 13th century, the collection of tiny workshop villages which clustered around the palace walls evolved into craft cooperatives, or guilds. Skilled craftsmen migrated to the Quarter, and artisan guilds were formed by craftsmen originating from the same village and performing similar services.

Members of the guilds worked and lived together, creating a cooperative system for transporting merchandise to the designated streets in the business quarter.

Because inhabitants of each street came from the same village, streets developed a homogeneous look. Commoners' homes evolved out of market stalls, before streets were formed. Because storekeepers were taxed according to the width of their storefront, storage and living space moved to the rear of the buildings. Consequently, the long and narrow buildings were called "tube houses." Typical measurements for such houses are 3 meters wide by 60 meters long.

The Old Quarter has a rich religious heritage. When the craftsmen moved from outlying villages into the capital, they brought with them their religious practices. They transferred their temples, pagodas and communal houses to their new location. Each guild has one or two religious structures and honors its own patron saint or founder. Therefore, on each street in the Old Quarter there is at least one temple. Now, many of the old temples in the Old Quarter have been transformed into shops and living quarters, but some of the old buildings' religious roots can still be recognized by the architecture of their roofs.

Although the old section of Hanoi is often called the "36 Old Streets," there are more than 36 actual streets. Some researchers believe that the number 36 came from the 15th century when there might have been 36 guild locations, which were workshop areas, not streets. When streets were later developed, the guild names were applied to the streets. Others attribute the 36 to a more abstract concept. The number nine in Asia represents the concept of "plenty." Nine times the four directions makes 36, which simply means "many." There are now more than 70 streets in the area.

Some streets have achieved fame by their inclusion in popular guidebooks. Han Gai Street offers silk clothing ready-made and tailored, embroidery, and silver products. Hang Quat, the street that formerly sold silk and feather fans, now stuns the visitor by its brilliantly colored funeral and festival flags and religious objects and clothing. To Thinh Street connects the above two and is still the wood turner's street. Hang Ma glimmers with shiny paper products, such as gift wrappings, wedding decorations and miniature paper objects to burn for the dead. Lan Ong Street is a sensual delight of textures and smells emanating from the sacks of herbal medicinal products: leaves, roots, barks, and powders

In the early 13th century, the collection of tiny workshop villages which clustered around the palace walls evolved into craft cooperatives, or guilds.

The Old Quarterbegan to acquire its reputation as a crafts area when the Vietnamese attained independence in the 11th century and King Ly Thai To built his palace there. In the early 13th century, the collection of tiny workshop villages which clustered around the palace walls evolved into craft cooperatives, or guilds. Skilled craftsmen migrated to the Quarter, and artisan guilds were formed by craftsmen originating from the same village and performing similar services. Members of the guilds worked and lived together, creating a cooperative system for transporting merchandise to the designated streets in the business quarter.

Because inhabitants of each street came from the same village, streets developed a homogeneous look. Commoners' homes evolved out of market stalls, before streets were formed. Because storekeepers were taxed according to the width of their storefront, storage and living space moved to the rear of the buildings. Consequently, the long and narrow buildings were called "tube houses." Typical measurements for such houses are 3 meters wide by 60 meters long.

The Old Quarter has a rich religious heritage. When the craftsmen moved from outlying villages into the capital, they brought with them their religious practices. They transferred their temples, pagodas and communal houses to their new location. Each guild has one or two religious structures and honors its own patron saint or founder. Therefore, on each street in the Old Quarter there is at least one temple. Now, many of the old temples in the Old Quarter have been transformed into shops and living quarters, but some of the old buildings' religious roots can still be recognized by the architecture of their roofs.

Although the old section of Hanoi is often called the "36 Old Streets," there are more than 36 actual streets. Some researchers believe that the number 36 came from the 15th century when there might have been 36 guild locations, which were workshop areas, not streets. When streets were later developed, the guild names were applied to the streets. Others attribute the 36 to a more abstract concept. The number nine in Asia represents the concept of "plenty." Nine times the four directions makes 36, which simply means "many." There are now more than 70 streets in the area.

Some streets have achieved fame by their inclusion in popular guidebooks. Han Gai Street offers silk clothing ready-made and tailored, embroidery, and silver products. Hang Quat, the street that formerly sold silk and feather fans, now stuns the visitor by its brilliantly colored funeral and festival flags and religious objects and clothing. To Thinh Street connects the above two and is still the wood turner's street. Hang Ma glimmers with shiny paper products, such as gift wrappings, wedding decorations and miniature paper objects to burn for the dead. Lan Ong Street is a sensual delight of textures and smells emanating from the sacks of herbal medicinal products: leaves, roots, barks, and powders.

Some streets in Old Quarter

-Hang Bac Street

A majority of the street names in the Old Quarter start with the word hang. Hang means merchandise or shop. The guild streets were named for their product, service or location. Hang Bac, one of the oldest streets in Vietnam, dates from at least the 13th century. Bac means silver, and appropriately, this street started as a silver ingot factory under the reign of Le Thanh Tong (1469-1497). Village people, called the "Trau Khe silver casters," were brought into the capital to cast silver bars and coins. After a ceremony to transfer their craft from their village of Trau Khe to Hanoi, they set up two temples to honor the founders of their craft. At one communal house, the silver was molten and poured into molds. At the other communal house, the molds were further processed for delivery to the Prime Minister. The crafters went to great lengths to keep their methods secret to avoid counterfeit products.

At the turn of the 18th century, the street took on more varied functions. In addition to the casting of silver ingots, the street attracted more jewelry makers and money exchangers. Money exchangers thrived, since in the old days, paper money was not used. Instead, currency consisted of bronze and zinc coins and silver ingots. When merchants needed a large amount of money for business transactions, they would exchange the heavy metal bars on Hang Bac.

During the French time it was called "Exchange Street." Although paper currency was later used, the word for it included the word bac.

Hang Bac also has jewelers of different types: engravers, smelters, polishers, and gold-leaf makers. The first jewelry makers were the Dong Cac guild, which settled during the Le dynasty (1428-1788). They founded a temple dedicated to three brothers who learned their art in China in the 6th century, and who are considered the patron saints of the Vietnamese jewelry making profession.

There are several famous buildings on this street. In the communal house on Hang Bac, there is a stone stele, built in 1783, telling about a Mandarin who forcibly took over the communal house. The locals took him to court and won back their building. The Dung Tho Temple is dedicated to Chu Bi, a Taoist deity. At the end of the French colonial period, this temple had been named Truong Ca, after a person who watched over the temple and served the best noodle soup. One building on this street is the pride of contemporary history-the Chuong Vang (Golden Bell) Theater, which still hosts traditional Vietnamese theater performances. The former traditional-venue theater, the To Nhu (Quang Lac) Theater built in the 1920s, also is on this street but has been transformed into apartments.

-Hang Be Street
In the mid-19th century, the guild of bamboo raft makers was located on this street outside the My Loc gate, one of the many sturdy gates

to the city. The cai mang raft consisted of 12 to 15 large bamboo poles lashed together by strips of green bamboo bark. Their anterior was slightly raised by heating the wood, and the aft was rigged with three quadrangular sails made of coarse linen dyed with extracts of sweet potato skins.

Bamboo rafts were sensible for Hanoi's shallow rivers, lakes and swamps, which can not provide solid anchorage or natural shelter from storms. The flat design better weathered the seasonal typhoons that lash the northern part of Vietnam, and is better adapted to coastal and river fishing. The bamboo poles from which the rafts were constructed were sold one block east on Hang Tre Street.

-Cau Go Street
Meaning "Wooden Bridge," Cau Go Street is located one block north of the Lake of the Restored Sword, and was in fact the location of a wooden bridge. About 150 years ago, the bridge crossed a thin stream of water connecting the Thai Cuc Lake with the Lake of the Restored Sword. Dyers from the neighboring Silk Street set out their silk to dry or bleached their fabric beside the bridge. Under the French occupation, the lake and stream were filled as health measures and to increase buildable land. The little wooden bridge became a regular street.

On the edge of the lake, women in wide brimmed hats once sold armfuls of flowers to the French for a few coins. Today a flower market exists where the Cau Go alley intersects with the main street. Other historical sites on Cau Go are the secret headquarters and hiding place of the 1930-45 "Love the Country" resistance movement.

Cau Gotoday is a commercial street specializing in women's accessories.

-Hang Dao Street
This street is one of Vietnam's oldest streets. It serves as a main axis running from north to south, cutting the Old Quarter in half. In the French Colonial time, Hang Dao Street was a center for the trading of silk products. On the first and sixth days of the lunar month, there were fairs for the sale of silk items. Shops also sold other types of fabric such as gauze, brocade, crepe, and muslin. Almost all the non-silk products were white.

In the beginning of the 15th century, this street was the location of the silk dyer guild from the Hai Hung Province, which specialized in a deep pink dye. Dao, the name of the street, refers to the pink of apricot blossoms, which are symbolic of the Vietnamese Lunar New Year. The demand for this special color was so high that the fabric had to be dyed at other locations as well.

Hang Thiec is the street of tinsmiths. The craftsmen originally produced small tin cone-shaped tips which were used to preserve the shape of the traditional conical hats

By the 18th century, the dye colors diversified. In the 18th-century work Notes About the Capital, the author wrote that "Hang Dao guild does dying work. It dyes red as the color of blood, black as Chinese ink, and other beautiful colors."

In the 19th century, Hang Dao was lined by about 100 houses, of which only 10 or so were constructed of bricks. The rest were of thatch. On the side of the street alongside the now filled-in Hang Dao Lake, the foundations of the houses have visibly sunk lower than the road.

By the turn of this century, Indian textile merchants opened shops for trading silk and wool products imported from the West. This street now specializes in ready-made clothing.

-Dong Xuan Street/ Market Street
This street originally belonged to two villages-the even numbered houses were occupied by the Nhiem Trung village, and the odd numbered houses were occupied by the Hau Tuc village.

The Dong Xuan market, Vietnam's oldest and largest market, occupies half of the street.

River networks formed the economic hub of Hanoi by providing a system of waterways which fed the city and markets. Located at the confluence of the To Lich and Red Rivers, the Dong Xuan market was once one of the busiest urban areas in Southeast Asia.

The French required merchants to bring their goods inside the fenced perimeter of the market in order to facilitate tax collections. When the number of merchants swelled, the market was enlarged. In 1889, a structure was built over it, and five gates were built leading to it. Each of the five market gates was used only for specified goods. In 1992, the market was renovated and a new facade erected.

-Hang Mam Street
Hang Mamis the union of two old streets: an eastern offshoot called Hang Trung and the original Hang Mam. The name is derived from the various kinds of mam, or fish sauces, that are produced and sold here, as well as other sea products. The street was originally on the riverside, close to the day's catch.

Nuoc mam, or fish sauce, is made from fish that are too small to be sold individually which are placed in clay vats with water and salt. Boiled water is poured over the fish and weights are placed on top of the mixture to compress it. The concoction distills for days, and the result is a clear amber juice that is rich in protein, vitamins and minerals. With aging, the fierce ammoniac odors of the fish become mellow, and like brandy, the flavor improves. The first pressing, which is the clearest and purest, is called nuoc mam nhi, or prime. The sauce was stored in barrels made on adjacent Hang Thung Street.

In the 1940s, new specialties appeared on the street. A small ceramics industry appeared along with those of memorial stone etching, coffin, and tombstone manufacturers.

-Ma May Street

This street also is a union of two old streets. Hang May sold rattan products, and Hang Ma sold sacred joss (paper replicas of money, clothing, even stereo sets) to burn for the dead. Ma is burned in front of the altar of ancestors accompanied by prayers. Around the turn of the century, the streets became one: Ma May.

On the edge of the lake, women in wide brimmed hats once sold armfuls of flowers to the French for a few coins.

In the French time, this street was called "Black Flag Street" because the soldier Luu Vinh Phuc had his headquarters here. Luu was the leader of the Black Flags, a bandit unit operating around Hanoi in the late 19th century. They were essentially pirates who made a living robbing villagers and merchants. In the 1880s, the Black Flags cooperated with the Vietnamese Imperial Forces to resist the French who were attempting to gain military control of Hanoi.

In the middle of the street is the Huong Tuong temple, established in 1450, which honors Nguyen Trung Ngan (1289-1370), a governor of Thang Long, the former name of Hanoi.

-Hang Thiec Street

Hang Thiec is the street of tinsmiths. The craftsmen originally produced small tin cone-shaped tips which were used to preserve the shape of the traditional conical hats. A neighboring street, Hang Non, made the hats, and both streets comprised the Yen No hamlet.

Hang Thiec Street also produced oil lamps, candle sticks, and opium boxes. Tin shops sold mirrors, which they still do today, along with sheet metal, zinc, and glass. The street echoes busily with the clanging of hammers against the sheet metal. Workers spread out on the sidewalk shaping metal storage boxes and other objects to custom order.

-Hang Thung Street
In the old days, on this block inside the Dong Yen gate, barrels were manufactured. The barrels were used for storing and carrying water and fish sauce. The communal house and the temple of the barrel makers' guild is located at 22 Hang Thung, but is hidden behind newer buildings. The street is shaded by the leaves of the xoan tree which has a fluffy cream colored cluster flower and bright red berries. The tree has various English names: Margosa, Bead, or China Berry tree. In May, the tiny flowers fall to the ground like yellow confetti. The furrowed bark is often scraped off by local residents, who dry and boil it to make a medicinal infusion as a vermifuge.

The Old Quarter is a precious legacy of Hanoi's ancient past, but the area is challenged by rapid changes.

Today, handicraft production is increasingly replaced by restaurants, repair shops, and mini hotels. Historic buildings have become mass living spaces and schools as the population increases. Craft workers now constitute nine percent of the neighborhood. Traders make up 40 percent. With the new economic policies, a dramatic building boom has begun, threatening the charm of the district. Local, national, and international agencies are now formulating plans to preserve the historic ambiance of the Old Quarter. Meaning of the 36 streets (just old name but in fact more than there)

Tourism

Safety in Hanoi

Hanoi remains a relatively safe city for visitors, but being aware of some typical hazards will increase the likelihood of you having a hassle-free stay. Here are some things to beware of.

Petty theft is not be a big issue in Hanoi, but bear in mind that the average Vietnamese salary is around $150 per month. The wealth disparity is broad, meaning a hell of a lot of people earn far less than that, even in cities like Hanoi. This might make your iPod, cash, camera and jewellery an enticing prospect, so it makes sense to take basic precautions to avoid being a target for thieves.

Don't carry too much cash. Use an ATM card for regular withdrawals or keep the cash in a safety deposit box at your hotel. When out and about keep your cash and passport safely tucked away in a money belt and other items in a zipped up bag which is over your shoulder so it's not easy to rip off. Rucksacks are okay if you're on the move, but can be sliced open when on public transport or standing in a crowd.

Be especially vigilant at night when the streets are quieter and it's easier for thieves to cut and run, particularly when victims are drunk. We're not saying don't drink but if you're planning a big night out don't take valuables, make sure you're with other people and do have a plan for how you're getting back to your hotel, particularly if you head outside Old Quarter to areas like Phuc Tan (where the infamous Phuc Tan Club is located).

Violent crime is not a grave concern either, but we have heard recent reports about single women expats being followed home and even physically attacked. Avoid wandering the streets at night, especially alone. We've also heard of taxi passengers being threatened when they refuse to pay inflated fares or when they comment that the meter's running too fast. If you are going to cause a fuss about the meter and we wouldn't blame you try to wait until you're at your destination and have an escape route and other people around you.

If you do find yourself a victim of theft or violence, we've got some pointers on loss, theft and the police.

The main hazard to be aware of in Hanoi is the roads and pavements, or anywhere else traffic chooses to drive, legal or not. Whether walking or driving, Hanoi's roads are dangerous. It may seem like everything is moving effortlessly in a flow but accidents do happen especially outside slow-moving Old Quarter. You've heard this before, but when crossing roads walk slowly and steadily in a line with your companions, but keep your eyes open too! Yes, people will drive round you, but many people are on mobile phones or just not looking so you also need to remain alert and ready to adjust your pace in an emergency.

Don't trust red lights, pedestrian crossings or one-way streets: motorbikes and even four-wheeled vehicles regularly ignore traffic signals in an effort to shave a few minutes off their journey. This includes driving on pavements and through parks.

If you are going to rent a motorbike to drive yourself, observe the driving style of Hanoians first and make sure you are confident on the bike before venturing too far. Vietnam has one of the highest road fatality rates in the world and estimates of annual fatalities range from 10,000 to 20,000 per year. Don't think it won't happen to you. Don't drink and drive, wear a helmet and take it easy. And don't forget, if you don't have a local license your insurance won't cover you in case of an accident.

A minor motorbike related consideration: exhaust pipes are hot. Be careful not to brush against them as you navigate parked motorbikes a burn hurts.

As for drink and drugs, we have not heard of any incidents of tourists being affected by dodgy alcohol, but there have been some deaths among locals due to contaminated rice wine and vodka. Drugs are available you know the risks to both your health and your freedom.

Men should be aware of being courted by sex workers; do remember that HIV is an issue here, as is stealing from flattered and satisfied clients.

Hanoi has seen a few outbreaks of diseases recently: Japanese encephalitis and measles have caused deaths among Vietnamese, particularly children. Dengue is also a risk, as is rabies. None of these are at epidemic levels but do ensure you're inoculated and wear mosquito repellant, or cover up, to avoid bites.

Avoiding scams in Hanoi

Hanoi is probably known for being home to more scams than average in Southeast Asia. Here's what to watch out for to help you avoid them.

First, let's get some definitions agreed, as I feel the word "scam" is overused. A scam is not someone trying to charge you 100,000 VND for a silk scarf when you know your friend bought one for 50,000 VND yesterday that's just good business sense, and you can always say no. A scam is someone doing something wrong/illegal/underhand in order to cheat someone out of money.

Based on that definition the main scams in Hanoi involve transport particularly taxis to and from transport hubs like stations and airports. They're scams because you are being blatantly overcharged and cheated by dodgy meters, or by drivers deliberately taking long routes or going to the wrong hotel.

Exchange rates

One scam to watch for is the exchange rate con. Unscrupulous hotels quote rates in dollars, then when you want to pay in dong, inflate the exchange rate well up. For a long stay, this can really sting. It's easily countered, however. Before booking, if possible, ask the price in the currency you are going to pay in. If you've pre-booked, then check again when you arrive. If the rate is too high, then get that out in the open before you hand over your passport or any other guarantee. Alternatively, pay in the currency they've quoted usually dollars. In any case, carefully check your bill before paying up.

Other hotel issues

So the hotel puts you in a room with a broken shower/ cracked TV/ripped bedding, and then when you go to check out they try to charge you for the damage. Avoid this by ensuring you inform reception immediately of any damage when you check into a room. If you're at all suspicious of their motives or attitude, get them to write it down, or fix it straight away.

Also and this isn't just related to the above scam try to avoid leaving your passport as a deposit. If things get nasty for any reason, it's easier to walk away if they're not holding your passport. Instead, if they need a guarantee, pay in advance you might lose a bit of cash but that's nowhere near as much hassle as losing your passport.

And make sure you do your research on the hotel you're staying at first so you don't end up suffering the same fate as those before you.

Tours

Tours can sometimes cause problems. For instance, hotels and travel agents may sell you a "deluxe" Halong Bay tour which is certainly not deluxe, or use fake photos to present a rosier image than the reality. The only way to avoid this is to get recommendations from other travellers or online and shop around, but it's still a tricky area and one that has no fail-safe solution. This applies for tours and travel booking the rates that agents charge for train tickets is far higher than the face value and varies by quite a bit between agents.

Over-charging

Although it's important to differentiate between scams and general over-charging when you can say no/negotiate/go elsewhere being over-charged for something you don't know the fair price of could be classified as a scam in some instances, such as visa extensions, when the agent or hotel wants US$50. Is that a reasonable price or expensive?

Visa prices change regularly, and differ by nationality and other factors so make sure you shop aroundrather than accepting the first price you get. In theory it's possible to go to Immigration and do it yourself, but we recommend you pay a bit extra for an agent to do it for you.

Avoiding taxi scams in Hanoi

Taxi cheats are probably the one thing travellers to Hanoi complain most about. While unlikely to cost you a fortune, it's still annoying to be over-charged or literally taken for a ride. So here's what to watch out for and how to avoid over-paying or ending up at a zero-star hotel in a back alley when you booked in at somewhere fancy.

Taxis from the airport

Noi Bai airport is often referenced as a hotbed of scamming taxi drivers and has been well-covered in the Travelfish.org forum. In theory, all the licensed metered cabs that wait at the rank should be charging the prices on the rate board. If you use one of these taxis, get agreement on the rate before you get in by pointing at the rates sign and getting a confirming nod. If the driver tries to charge you more upon arrival, don't pay. Also, don't pay any extras for the tolls/parking that is all included.

However, although in theory these taxis should be fine I've never had problems it's safest to book in advance, either through your hotel or a company such as Hanoi Airport Transfers. This is highly recommended if you're arriving late in the evening, once the buses have stopped running, as even the licensed, supposedly fixed rate taxis hike their rates up then.

For the budget-conscious, take the Jetstar or Vietnam Airlines buses into town they have a fixed rate. If these aren't around you can also try private minivans and public buses, but you are likely to be charged a little more than locals for the minivans only by maybe a dollar, but if that's going to bother you stick to the airline buses.

Whatever you do, do not get waylaid by the men who pounce when you leave arrivals; chances are they work for an unlicensed taxi firm and will overcharge.

As well as over-charging, apparently taxis from the airport or station (see below) often take people to the wrong hotel, as they are working on commission. Hotels will certainly tell you this is the case in order to persuade you to book a transfer with them, and of course this does avoid the issue. But if you've not booked a hotel or they're over-charging for the transfer (many do), make sure you have the exact name and address of the hotel you are heading for, ideally written down in Vietnamese, and make it clear to the driver that you have a reservation. There are often multiple hotels with the same name, but they don't all share an address. If the driver takes you somewhere else you have two options: (1) get out and walk (2) refuse to pay until they take you where you want to go.

Taxis from the train station

Tourists arriving on an overnight train, tired and unfamiliar with Hanoi and just wanting to get to their hotel? Easy prey for unscrupulous taxi drivers. There are usually a good number of Mai Linh taxis at the train station, parked on the platform, so go for one of those if you can but even they sometimes try to negotiate a high fixed rate, so insist on the meter.

If you don't get a Mai Linh then you'll walk out of the exit to a melee of taxi drivers offering you a ride. Dodgy meters which run too fast are a big problem at the train station, so it's one occasion where negotiating a fixed rate, even if it's a bit higher than the meter should be, is a good idea. As a rough guide, it's about two kilometres to the cathedral area, so 30,000-40,000 VND is a fair fixed price, depending upon the size of taxi. It's a bit further to Ma May area, so you'll likely need to pay 40,000-50,000 VND to get there.

If you decide to risk it with the meter and notice it's running too fast, threaten to get out (though you won't really want to as there won't be any other taxis around) and try to push for a fixed price. Drivers don't want to lose a fare as they'll likely have to wait for the next train for another one, so you're in a good position.

Note that there are a few one-way systems between the station and Old Quarter, so even if you know which direction you should be going, don't be surprised if it's not quite as direct as you expect.

Taxis around town

It's not just from the transport hubs that taxis try it on. I used to avoid getting taxis from Old Quarter home at that time home was in Ba Dinh, about five kilometres from Old Quarter because I was convinced they'd cheat me and I didn't want to have to deal with that, particularly late at night. Even now, I'm wary, but I'm more sussed so am able to avoid problems.

Taxis that service the Old Quarter are particularly at fault, but it happens elsewhere in the capital as well I took a taxi with three well-built guys from the *bia hoi* place on Tran Vu into Old Quarter a few months back and just a few kilometres down the road the meter was already on 50,000 VND with no sign of slowing. It should have been about 30,000 VND. "Stop!" we shouted and out we jumped, indicating our displeasure with his obvious dishonesty. On that occasion we didn't pay him a dime and he didn't argue, given the three well-built guys although for less blatant cheaters we'll usually pay what we think it's worth.

So, back to how to avoid a dodgy meter/long route/inflated fixed rate.

One option is to only use the well-regarded taxi companies. Mai Linh is always recommended, but Taxi Group and ABC are also solid though Taxi Group is pricier and I've never had any problems with the small Phu Dong, Thanh Nga, Vic or Morning taxis. But don't sue me if you do! They're sometimes in scant supply in Old Quarter so onto my second piece of advice: walk out of the tourist centre to pick up a taxi. If I'm in the Ma May area, I will walk to the main road.

Another is to get your hotel/the bar or restaurant you're at to call you a taxi. Most will be happy to do so. There's no guarantee it will be one of the recommended companies, but as long as you're at a reputable place it shouldn't be a problem. Ask them how much it should cost too, just to get an idea.

Agreeing a fixed rate is only advisable if you know how much you should be paying. Their first bid is likely to be high, especially late at night.

Alternatively, take another mode of transport. Walking is a great way to see Hanoi, buses run reasonably frequently, or combine travel with sightseeing on a cyclo.

My final tip regarding taxis, wherever you catch them, is to make sure you have enough change on you. It's a common trick for drivers to claim they don't have any change. If they do this, pay less rather than more (if you have it) no change, their problem, not yours.

Transportation
How to get to and from Hanoi

Getting from the airport into Hanoi

This trip gets bad press but if you know what's what and don't let a random taxi driver persuade you to pay them $20, you should be fine. Here are your options.

First up a word of caution: if you arrive on a late evening flight you'd be advised to book a taxi or hotel pick-up in advance as the buses stop running before the last flights and taxis get very cheeky, refusing to stick to the stated price.

The main rule is don't panic! Hanoi airport is actually very small and all of the transport options leave from directly outside the terminal. We've heard reports of unhelpful staff at the information desk refusing to explain where the buses go from. Ignore them and walk outside taxis and private minibuses are usually straight ahead or to the left and airline buses are to the right.

Private minibuses: Confirm the price first we paid 30,000 VND on our last trip and expect it to leave as soon as it is full, which usually doesn't take long. This option is popular with locals and the bus will stop off a few times to drop people off along the way. We can't guarantee where exactly you'll be dropped off, but it should be central enough to walk or take a short taxi ride to where you do want to go. Just be prepared to be flexible and don't expect any English to be spoken.

Airline transfer service:
Jetstar runs a transfer service for 30,000 VND in large, comfortable,

bright orange coaches. When we tried them, they dropped us off at the Sofitel Plaza near Truc Bach Lake upon request, but it continues on to their office on Tran Quang Khai to the east of Hoan Kiem lake. For the energetic it's possible to walk into town from here, but most will prefer to take a short taxi ride. Just be careful we've heard the taxis that pick up from here can be a bit dodgy so keep an eye on the meter

Vietnam Airlines also runs a transfer service for the same price. The disadvantage is that it's on a crowded minibus, but it has a convenient drop off on Quang Trung Street, just to the southwest of Hoan Kiem Lake and opposite their main office. With heavy bags you'll probably want to jump in a taxi from there to your hotel but if you're staying near St Joseph's Cathedral it's walkable. A taxi up to the centre of Old Quarter should only cost about 20,000 VND.

Taxi:

Unfortunately plenty of unscrupulous taxi drivers still prowl at the airport, waiting to pounce and over-charge, so if you are approached by an individual driver, politely say no and make your way outside to the official taxi ranks. A few different companies operate and they have a board up listing prices it should cost 380,000 VND for a standard four-seater car (not per person!). Don't pay any more. You buy a ticket at the stand for the posted price and wait in the line. This price should include the toll, so don't pay extra for it.

A few more tips to avoid getting ripped off:

(a) Write down the address, exact name and phone number of your hotel before you get into the cab. If the driver tells you it's closed or full, insist on confirming that for yourself, and be sure to check the address when checking the hotel. Be assertive.

(b) Book a taxi in advance with an operator like Hanoi Airport Transfers, which you can call (+84 912 881 885) or email (info@hanoiairporttransfer.com) in advance, or book through their website. Or try Noi Bai Taxis (04 3886 5615).

(c) If you suspect you're being given a bum steer, don't get angry. Just keep insisting on being taken where you want to go, and simply refuse to pay more than the agreed-upon price. The scammers rely on tourists being too polite and exhausted to put up a fight.

(f) Almost everyone gets ripped off a little bit when they first arrive in Hanoi. Budget for it, and don't take it personally!

Airport pick-up:Most hotels will arrange this for you if you've pre-booked a room. They may charge a bit more than the taxis at the airport but the benefit is that there will be someone waiting for you at the airport and you're almost guaranteed to get taken to the right hotel but as this is Hanoi, do still be sure to check you've been taken to the correct address upon arrival.

Public bus:We've not taken a public bus from the airport into town but this is the cheapest way to do it. The Numbers 7 and 17 both pick up at Arrivals and cost 5,000 VND the price should be printed on the outside of the bus, by the door. Be warned the driver may not have any change if you only have large notes.

The Number 7 terminates at Kim Ma bus station. Then it'll cost around 35,000 for a taxi, depending upon size of taxi and where you are heading, or take a motorbike taxi aim for 20,000 but be prepared to pay 30,000. The Number 17 terminates at Long Bien bus station. This is to the north of Old Quarter and about a 20-minute walk to the hotels on that side of town, or a short taxi ride.

Getting from Hanoi to Noi Bai International Airport

Getting back to the airport of course offers a fairly similar array of options.

Public bus: Again this is the cheapest but slowest option. Allow two hours' bus time before check-in. No. 7 picks up at Kim Ma bus station and 17 picks up along Tran Quang Khai at the eastern edge of the Old Quarter. Fare is 4,000/5,000 VND.

Airport shuttle: Next cheapest and by far the best option is one of the airport shuttles. The Vietnam Airlines shuttle generally starts at 04:30 and knocks off at around 19:00. But be careful, as if they don't have enough people at the scheduled time they sometimes wait another hour. Make sure you have money for a cab as an emergency back up to make your flight on time. Buses depart from 1 Quang Trung just south of Trang Thi, to the southwest of the lake and you can buy your ticket there, about $2. Jetstar picks up 206 Tran Quang Khai Street, to the east of Old Quarter. It's a big, more comfortable bus than the Vietnam Airlines option, and costs just 35,000 VND. They advise you arrive at the office two hours and 30 minutes before flight time and you can check in at the office.

Taxi: Taxis should cost around $12 per trip for up to four people if you can fit all your stuff in the cab with you. A seven-passenger car should be about $15-$20 and works out well if you have a lot of stuff or are in a big group.

Train

Hanoi's main train station is located not far from the centre of Hoan Kiem, on the border of Ba Dinh district on Le Duan Street. The easiest way to get here is to head west on Ly Thuong Kiet, which ends right at the station.

It's actually two stations: Station A for departures to the south, and Station B for the north. Although they're just across the tracks from each other, you can't walk between them you'll have to go via streets that take you around the block. This may come up, as trains scheduled to depart at one station are sometimes rerouted to the other for logistical reasons. Even if you're told exactly which station to go to, arrive early enough to switch stations. It only takes a few minutes, but the whole thing can be confusing.

Tourists mostly head to Station B for trains to Sapa, which has no station, but trains stop at the nearby town of Lao Cai, 40 kilometres away. Regular shuttles from Lao Cai station to Sapa cost about $2. Jeeps and moto-taxis are also available. Lao Cai is just under 300 kilometres from Hanoi, and the trip usually takes nine to 10 hours. Trains leave nightly at 20:35, 21:10 and 21:50 (the SP trains 7, 1 and 3) and arrive in Lao Cai at 4:55, 5:25 and 6:15 respectively. You'll be travelling in the dark so don't expect to see anything outside your window. But the great thing is you simply hop on board, tuck into your bunk, and when you wake up, you're there. The so-called 'hard sleepers' sound worse than they are; there's a thin mattress with a thick blanket and most travellers we've met have slept just fine using these. Prices for a hard sleeper bunk with air-con range from 355,000 to 450,000 VND and soft sleeper bunks with air-con from 515,000 VND.

You can book and catch trains south to Hue, Da Nang, Nha Trang, HCMC and other destinations in between from Station A. Southbound trains depart daily at 6:15, 15:45, 19:00, 21:55 and 23:00. Sample fair and trip times include:

<u>Hue</u>: Hard sleeper with air-con: 654,000–804,000 VND, soft sleeper with air-con: 840,000–850,000 VND, 13 hours
<u>Da Nang</u>: Hard sleeper with air-con: 724,000–890,000 VND, soft sleeper with air-con: 930,000–940,000 VND, 15.5 hours

Nha Trang: Hard sleeper with air-con: 1,250,000–1,536,000 VND, soft sleeper with air-con: 1,604,000–1,624,000 VND, 25.5 hours

Ho Chi Minh City: Hard sleeper with air-con: 1,355,000–1,666,000 VND, soft sleeper with air-con: 1,740,000–1,760,000 VND, 33 hours.

There is a departure from the central Hanoi station to Hai Phong at 06:00, but more originate from Long Bien, on the west side of the Red River, only about two kilometres from Hoan Kiem. You can buy tickets at the central station in Hanoi for these departures, but you'll need to be at Long Bien to catch your train, so make sure to double check. Or you can buy tickets at the Long Bien station itself for 65,000 VND or less from 05:00 to 21:00.

The Hai Phong trains from Long Bien are:
LP3 at 09:30 arriving 12:10
LP5 at 15:35 arriving 18:00
LP7 at 18:10 arriving 20:35

The Vietnamese government celebrates Tet (Lunar New Year) by raising the prices of all train tickets. It's different for each line, but the jump is about 10%, generally occurs two weeks before Tet and continues for a week or so afterwards. Book as far in advance as possible when travelling on or around Tet.

Trains to China

International trains between Beijing, China and Hanoi, Vietnam started up in 2008. Obviously, have your visa sorted out before you board. Take note that in Vietnamese, Beijing is Bac Kinh, and Nanning is Nam Ninh.

The Beijing trains run on Tuesdays and Fridays only and depart at 18:30 from the Hanoi Train Station A, arriving in Beijing two days (43 hours) later at about 12:00. It costs about $350.

These same trains stop at Nanning, 396 kilometres away, at 06:30 the next morning (12 hours) so you could break up the trip if you like. The fare is 1.5m VND.

But if you're going to Nanning, the daily trains out of Gia Lam station are much cheaper. The station is to the west on the other side of the Red River from Hoan Kiem district, a kilometre past the Chuong Duong bridge. Tickets cost 800,000 VND and the train departs at 21:40, arriving in Nanning at just after 09:00 the next morning.

All of these tickets can be booked at the station or at a travel agent, who will, of course, charge a small mark up.

When booking train tickets with a travel agent, you're generally not issued a ticket, but a voucher that will need to be exchanged with a tour company agent at the train station for an actual ticket. These agents hang out at the steps outside the staion. Show any one of them your voucher and they'll direct you to the person who will have your tickets. It's chaotic and confusing, but it works. Make sure to allow plenty of time prior to your departure to sort it all out.

Bus

Hanoi is a massive transportation hub, with four bus stations and three train stations of use to foreigners. Sorting out where to go to get where you want to go can be time consuming, so often you will be better off paying for the convenience of booking through a hotel or travel agency. The prices below should give a general idea of how much extra you're paying. Those who like to do it on their own may want to factor in transport to the station when calculating the overall price. You won't always do better than booking a ticket through a hotel and getting picked up in town. Gia Lam station is the most convenient to the Old Quarter, so depart from there if you have a choice.

My Dinh Bus Station

Ben Xe My Dinh T: (04) 3768 5549; ticketing open 04:30-23:00.
My Dinh is a seven kilometre trek to the west of town. There are departures to dozens of northern cities, and a number of destinations

to the south and east. Only the major destinations are listed below. To get here, take Tran Phu west from the Old Quarter, turn left at the end onto Son Tay and continue until it becomes Kim Ma. Keep going straight, following a roundabout to Cua Giay, continuing until the road crosses under an overpass. Take a left on to Pham Hung.

Bac Ha: Departs at 07:15, 08:15 and 09:35, costs 180,000 VND.

Bac Kan (for Ba Be Nat'l Park): 05.50, 06.20, 13.30 and 15.30, costs 100,000–180,000 VND, 3.5 hours

Bai Chay (Halong Bay): Departures every 15 minutes from 05:30 to 18:00, costs 90,000 VND, 3 hours

Cao Bang: Departs 05:00-20:00 (15 departures), costs 117,000 VND, 10 hours

Dien Bien: Departures 04:30-19:00, costs 350,000 VND, 8 hours

Ha Giang: Departs 03:40-06:00, costs 200,000 VND, 8 hours

Hoa Binh: Departs 05:00-17:00 (30 departures), costs 40,000 VND, 2 hours

Lai Chau: Departures every 30 minutes 17:00-20:00, costs 300,000 VND, 10 hours

Lao Cai: Departs at 07:30, costs 200,000 VND, 10 hours

Mai Chau: Departs at 06:00, 07:30, 14:00 and 14:30, costs 70,000 VND, 4 hours

Mong Cai: Departs from 07:30 onwards (30 departures), 230,000 VND, 10 hours

Nho Quan (for Cuc Phuong Nat'l Park): Departs 06:00-16:00 (every 15 minutes), costs 80,000 to 100,000 VND, 3 hours

Ninh Binh: Departs 06:00, 09:00, 14:00 and 17:00, costs 60,000 VND, 3 hours

Son La: Departures 07:00-20:00, costs 190,000 VND, 7 hours

Thanh Hoa: Departs at 08:30, 10:05, 10:15, 14:30 and 19:30, costs 75,000 VND, 4 hours

Vinh: Departs 05:00-20:00 (every 10 minutes), costs 150,000 VND, 5.5 hours

Southern Bus Terminal

Ben Xe Phia Nam T: (04) 3864 1467, ticketing 05:00 to 18:00
The Southern Bus terminal is located 5 kilometres south of the Old Quarter on Duong Giai and is dominated by private operators running comfortable buses on long distance routes, including to Vientiane. Departures are available to the north and east as well as the south. Buses to the Central Highlands run via Ho Chi Minh City.

Ha Tinh: Departs 07:40, 15:30, 21:15 and 21:40. 130,000 to 160,000 VND. Various operators.

Ho Chi Minh City: First class sleeper bus, food service, departs at 09:30, 11:15, 12:00, 16:00 and 17:30, costs 875,000 / 920,000 VND. Operators: MaiLinh, (04) 3633 6699, http://www.mailinhexpress.vn/ and Hoang Long Asia, (0313) 920 920, http://www.hoanglongasia.com.

Hue/Da Nang: First class sleeper with food departs at 16:00, costs 340,000 VND. First class seated with food departs at 17:00, costs 260,000 VND, 14 to 16 hours. Operator: Kim Chi, 0913 422 687

Quang Ngai: Departs 13:30 and 14:00, 370,000 VND. Operator: Chin Nghia, (0913) 422 687.

Quanh Binh: Departs 18:20, 170,000 VND. Operator: Xuat Ben, (0167) 828 2333.

Vientiene: Departs Tuesday, Thursday and Saturday at 19:00 and 19:30, 550,000 VND.

Vinh: Departs 08:20, 09:20, 15:00, 19:30, 21:00, 170,000 VND.

Gia Lam Bus Station

Ben Xe Gia Lam T: (04) 3827 1529, ticketing 05:00 to 18:00

This station is located east of the Red River on Ngo Gia Kham, two kilometres from the far side of the Chuong Duong or Long Bien Bridges. To get here, take either bridge then find Pho Ngoc Lam which runs east-west between the two bridges. Less than two kilometres later a sign indicates a right turn for the bus station and a left turn for the train station.

Hai Phong: Departs from 07:00 to 18:00 every hour except at 12:00. Costs 70,000 VND, takes 2 hours

Hon Gai (Halong City): Departs 06:00-16:00, every 20 minutes, costs

115,000 VND, takes 4 hours

<u>Lao Cai</u>: Departs at 18:00, costs 300,000 VND

<u>Lang Son</u>: Departs every 30 minutes from 06:00 to 12:00, costs 90,000 VND and takes 5 hours

<u>Mong Cai</u>: 12 departures from 06:00 to 19:00, costs 230,000 VND and takes 9 hours

<u>Thai Binh</u>: Departs at 10:30 and 14:30, costs 65,000 VND.

Buses to Laos

Nightly buses depart at 18:30 for Vientiane and you may be able to arrange hotel pickup. Tickets can be booked at most hotels and travel agencies, cost $35 for the 22-hour trip, and you'll have to have your Laos visa in advance. You'll save about $7 by buying direct (buses depart from the Southern Bus Terminal).

The roads are fine until you reach Laos proper, at which point things slow down considerably, and accidents have happened. There used to be through-buses, but our understanding is that at this point, you'll probably have to change buses at the border, and might even have to pay more money at that point, since if you don't, you'll be stranded in the middle of nowhere. So fly if you possibly can, and if going by land, any route you pick beside the one straight from Hanoi (or Dong Ha or Vinh) directly to Vientiane is a better choice. There are currently no through buses to Luang Prabang.

Buses to China

Through buses to China depart across the street from the Hong Ha Tourism office, at the hotel of the same name, on the west side of the Red River, along Tran Quang Khai. The buses have air-con and make frequent bathroom and food stops. Tickets cost $30. Purchase a day in advance and have your Chinese visa ready. Buses depart at 07:30 and 09:30, arriving in Nanning at 15:00 and 17:00 respectively the same day.

Hong Ha Tourism 204 Tran Quang Khai T: (04) 3824 7339

Getting around

Short trips within Hanoi on a xe om (motorcycle taxi) run 10,000 VND at a minimum. Metered taxis are also widely available, and often come out cheaper than a xe om for short trips, though they are slower and can't dodge traffic as well. For two or more people, a taxi is always cheaper than multiple xe oms.

It's pretty much understood that foreigners renting cyclos aren't really headed anywhere, they're just joyriding, and 100,000 VND per hour is quite sufficient compensation for your hard-working pedaller. You can bargain them down lower, but then you have to live with yourself. If you want to call a cab to pick you up, try Mai Linh at (04) 3861 6161 or

Hanoi Taxi at (04) 3253 5353.

The following fares are approximate, priced from Hanoi's old quarter:

By xe om

My Dinh Bus Station: 50,000 VND

Long Bien Train Station: 20,000 VND

Luong Yen Bus Station: 30,000 VND

Hanoi Train Station: 30,000 VND

Southern Bus Station: 50,000 VND

Gia Lam Bus/Train Station: 40,000 VND

By taxi

My Dinh Bus Station: 120,000 VND

Long Bien Train Station: 30,000 VND

Luong Yen Bus Station: 50,000 VND

Hanoi Train Station: 40,000 VND

Southern Bus Station: 70,000 VND

Gia Lam Bus/Train Station: 70,000 VND

Motorbike rentals

Motorbike rentals are affordable and easy to find just look for the signs in English on Dinh Liet or Hang Bac. The standard rate is $5 a day, or $50 a month for a 100 CC Honda wave or something like it. They'll usually keep your passport in lieu of a deposit. If your hotel is holding on to yours, have the rental agent call the hotel and sort it out.

If you're thinking of heading out of town on a motorbike trek, and you've been dreaming of riding a Minsk, we recommend you head to Hanoi Minsk Motorcycles on Luong Ngoc Quyen right next to the Irish Wolfhound. You can rent or buy bikes here, and what you see in the small shop is just the tip of the iceberg they have access to dozens more off site. If you're headed on a long trip, they'll want a deposit, which is fair enough, but if you're just tooling around town a passport is acceptable collateral. English is spoken and they really seem to love what they do. You'll find other shops scattered along Dinh Liet, Hang Bac and associated side streets. Currently, you don't need any kind of licence to rent if you're a foreigner, but keep an eye out as that may change, and if you cause an accident, it becomes an expensive issue to resolve.

Hanoi Minsk
4 Luong Ngoc Quyen. T: (04) 3926 4214. ngqhop@yahoo.com Hours: 08:00-18:00

Public buses
Hanoi Bus runs a comprehensive and very affordable public bus system throughout the city (and out to the airport). The buses are all

numbered and ply some very handy routes. If you pick up a tourist map in Hanoi, make sure it is one that marks the bus routes on it. You can check out their website for detailed bus route information.

Attractions

Temples

Hoe Nhai Pagoda

Hoe Nhai Pagoda was a major Buddhist pagoda under the Ly Dynasty and today offers a serene retreat from the busy city at its gates.

The dynasty ran from the 11th to 13th centuries, when it was set on a much larger plot of land. It was trimmed to its present more modest size when the French colonised Vietnam. One of the steles found here dates to the early 18th century, and allowed for historians to locate the site of the victory of Thang Long (now Hanoi) over the Mongols in 1258.

The pagoda is noted for a Buddha statue sitting on the back of a kneeling king. Legend has it that after King Le Hy Tong exiled Buddhist monks, one monk explained the tenets of Buddhism to him, and he was converted, thus ordering the statue to show his gratitude.

One Pillar Pagoda

Located in Ba Dinh Square right by the Ho Chi Minh Museum, the One Pillar Pagoda is one of the most recognisable symbols of Hanoi.

Having said that, it's not much to actually see in person. It's a modest, wooden sanctuary set on, naturally, one concrete pillar, over a pond that blooms with lotus blossoms during summer. The shrine is dedicated to Quan Am, the Goddess of Mercy, and is designed to look like a lotus, a symbol of enlightenment in Buddhism.

The pagoda is said to have originally been built in 1049 by Emperor Ly Thai Tong (who preceded Ly Thanh Tong, who was responsible for founding the Temple of Literature in 1070). Legend holds that the emperor, lacking male heirs, had a dream that he was handed a son by Quan Am, who was seated on a lotus flower when she appeared to him. Soon afterwards, the emperor found a wife and had a son. The emperor then built the pagoda to honour the goddess.

Today it contains a statue of her and sculptures of lotus flowers. Worshippers and you'll find plenty of them here climb a short flight of concrete steps to see the statue and make their offerings. The One Pillar Pagoda is popular with childless couples and is also believed to have miraculous healing powers.

Of course, the original pagoda no longer stands. It was most recently vandalised and burned by the French in 1954 as they retreated from Hanoi, only to be rebuilt by the Communist government.

Ngoc Son Temple

In the northern part of Hoan Kiem Lake, and accessed from the eastern side, sits Ngoc Son Pagoda, or Pagoda of the Jade Mountain, first used as a site of worship in the 14th century.

To get to the pagoda, you'll cross The Huc, or Rising Sun, bridge, a beautiful red wooden structure built in 1885 in classic Vietnamese style, and one of Hanoi's most iconic images. Then you'll find various little buildings on the island, including an outdoor area with space for just relaxing to take in the lake-side breeze and the colourful crowd for crowded it usually is.

At the entrance to the bridge are two monuments constructed in 1864, one representing an ink brush (a nine-metre tower) and the other an inkwell (a hollow rock held by three frogs). In the early morning of the festival of Doan Ngo, held on the fifth day of the fifth month, the shadow of the brush is positioned at the centre of the inkwell. The Chinese characters on the ink brush announce it's an instrument to write on the sky.

The pretty site surrounded by water has been used as a temple since ancient times, but most of the current structures here were built during the 19th century. It offers an eclectic variety of forefathers for Vietnamese to pay homage to, such as Confucian and Taoist notables, as well as intellectual Van Xuong, national hero General Tran Hung Dao, who defeated invading Mongols in the 13th century, La To, patron saint of doctors, and Quan Vu, a martial arts expert. It's a testament to how ancestor worship trumps Buddhism in the belief system of the average Vietnamese pagoda-goer.

There are various altars where the devoted worship by lighting incense and making offerings, and resident calligraphers were here when we last visited

Temple of Literature

The tranquil and sprawling Temple of Literature was established in 1070 by Emperor Ly Thanh Tong, and became the site of Vietnam's first university, the Imperial Academy or Quoc Tu Giam, six years later.

Today the grounds make for an interesting wander and step back into history, though the buildings are much newer after repeated renovations over the centuries.

Set on a large, rectangular complex encompassing five walled courtyards connected by gateways, among green gardens sprinkled with hanging orchids and featuring reflecting pools, the temple is something of a retreat from the hustle on the streets outside.

The temple features on Vietnam's 100,000 dong note and was dedicated to the cult of Confucius, which broke the monopoly over education previously held by Buddhism. The layout is similar to that of the temple at Confucius' birthplace, Qufu in Shandong. Initially mandarins and high-ranking civil servants were educated at the university, typically for three to seven years, but later outstanding students of no particular rank were also educated here.

After walking through the entrance gate and a large manicured garden, once used by scholars to relax in, visitors reach the Well of Heavenly Clarity, beside which are 82 of an original 117 turtles (representing wisdom) carrying stellae listing the names, places of birth and achievements of graduate students who accomplished exceptional results during the Le Dynasty, which started in 1484. The names on some of the stellae have been scratched out these are scholars who subsequently met with some sort of disgrace or royal disapproval, and were expunged from the record. In 1802, Emperor Gia Long transferred the national university to the new capital, Hue.

In modern times students used to come to rub the heads of the turtles for good luck ahead of their exams, but the turtles have now been roped off

Tran Quoc Pagoda

Tran Quoc Pagoda, the oldest pagoda in Hanoi, offers beautiful architecture, historic artifacts and a peaceful and serene environment.

Built in the sixth century during the reign of King Ly Nam De, the pagoda was first named Khai Quoc, which means "founding the country". Since then it has undergone a move, refurbishment and numerous name changes, but it remains a serene place to visit.

It was first constructed on the other side of the dyke road, by the river, but was moved in the 17th century to its current location on West Lake. Clearly the builders recognised what a prime piece of real estate Duong Thanh Nien was and that the lakeside location would add to the beauty to the pagoda.

The Buddhist pagoda is accessed via a short causeway lined with palm trees. The causeway leading to the temple gives a sense of drama as you approach, suggesting something of value lies ahead. The large entrance gate is one of the most recent additions, built in 1815, and through that to the left is a tall tower visible from the street. Entrance is free to the temple, but donations are encouraged.

The tower stands 15 metres high and has 11 tiers, each designed to represent the petals of a lotus flower. Each level has six arch windows containing a statue of Amitabha and on top of the tower sits a lotus flower made from precious stone but you can't get a good view of that from 15 metres below.

Brick-built shrines of all shapes and sizes surround the tower, most with incense wafting out from small windows or altars, and some with Chinese writing on the side; we can't tell you the meaning of these texts, but they are pretty.

You'll also see al pond containing a towering mountain of rock and topped with a statue of Goddess of Mercy Kuan Yin, and a yellow pagoda, construction dated 1939, which houses 14 engraved plaques chronicling the refurbishments

Pho Linh Tay Ho Pagoda

Pho Linh Tay Ho Pagoda in Hanoi's Tay Ho district is a fine example of a Vietnamese pagoda, with both traditional Buddhist symbolism and Tibetan statues and imagery.

The first area you come to as you enter the pagoda is the newer part of the complex. Here you will see both <u>statues and murals reflecting Tibetan Buddhism</u>, set around an open courtyard. Tibet is considered the closest place to Vietnam from which Buddhism came, so many temples in Vietnam are now incorporating Tibetan style.

As you continue your walk, with the lotus pond on your left particularly beautiful in lotus season the imagery becomes somewhat darker: along the wall the 10 deadly sins are represented, along with their gruesome punishments.

The walkway opens up into the temple courtyard, a peaceful spot in which to relax overlooking the pond, should the mood take you. The main building is at the end on the right. If as when we visited the doors are closed, try to get in round the back way, through the door that's up the steps from the courtyard. The staff were quite accommodating when we took this approach. Don't forget to take your shoes off though, whichever way you enter.

Inside is a shrine with representations of Buddha in each of the phases of his human life: he tried many different ways to reach Nirvana and these are represented by statues, including emaciated Buddha. The fat Buddha near the front symbolises what Nirvana may look or feel like, representing complete fulfilment. At the back is Buddha reaching enlightenment.

The gold statue in the centre depicts the dragons that protected Buddha at his birth. In Hinduism this would have been Naga, the seven-headed snake, but the Chinese changed this to dragons. Baby Buddha is at the front of the altar.

On either side of the altar are the angry and benign protectors, and in cases on the walls are the 10 judges of the 10 sins, as represented in the paintings outside.

As is common, the main building faces water in this case a large pond beside which is a shrine dedicated to the Goddess of Mercy, or Quan Am.

If you turn right when going up the stairs from the courtyard you will enter an enclosed yard. On the left is the accommodation building and directly opposite is another shrine dedicated to the three Mother Goddesses. You can see the Goddess of the Mountain's grotto on the left, with gaudy lighting and the cave of animals primarily tigers and deers a reflection of the animist beliefs of the time when the religion came to be.

How to get there

You can get to Pho Linh Tay Ho Pagoda (Chua) by heading down Dang Thai Mai Street from Xuan Dieu. The entrance to the pagoda is on the right between the lotus ponds. Consider combining a visit with a trip to Tay Ho Temple or Palace (Phu Tay Ho) which is about a 10-minute walk further down Dang Thai Mai Street and near to a number of eating places.

Pho Linh Tay Ho Pagoda

Dang Thai Mai St, Tay Ho District, Hanoi

Tay Ho Temple

One of the most popular and important places of worship in Hanoi, Tay Ho Temple trumps even Tran Quoc for its enviable lakeside position.

Phu Tay Ho is on the northern bank of the same-named lake, or West Lake, a few kilometres along the lake road from Xuan Dieu Street. Whereas pagodas are for Buddhists, Phu Ta Ho is dedicated to the Mother Goddesses and the Jade Emperor and is therefore most correctly referred to as a palace, although laypeople would call it a temple.

Don't just come straight into the temple. The street leading to the gate is packed with colourful stalls selling snacks like banh tom, prawns cooked on a thick batter base, then freshly re-fried before serving with a dipping sauce. You'll also find sweets, cakes, fruit, plus paraphernalia associated with making offerings at the temple, like fake money and incense. You will also see elderly men writing prayers for visitors to burn to send to the gods (or goddesses).

Legend has it that one of the three Mother Goddesses appeared to two Confucian scholars in a pub near the lake. She gave them food and drink and wrote poetry and they were so taken by her beauty that they later returned, but there was no sign of her or the pub, just a scroll of poetry, revealing herself as one of the Mother Goddesses. They then built the temple right next to the lake in her honour. Another variation of the legend says she appeared to a fisherman on the lake, smiling and reciting poetry

In the first large building you come to, if you turn left inside the gate, you will see three empty throne-like seats at the back of the altar. They represent the three Goddesses and are ready for the Goddesses to occupy when they are on earth. The altar in the building next door has effigies of the Goddesses, surrounded by their male Chinese servants. Below the altar is a cave of animals representing the animist set of beliefs in place at the time Mother Goddess

Tay Ho Temple

End of Dang Thai Mai St, Tay Ho District

06:00-19:00 daily; till 21:30 the 1st and 15th of each lunar month

Admission: Free

Bach Ma Temple

Bach Ma or White Horse Temple is beautiful, well-maintained and bustling, serving as a good example of what small temples in Vietnam are all about.

Reputed to be Hanoi's oldest temple, it was originally built in the ninth century by King Ly Thai To to worship Bach Ma. The white horse is said to have helped the king out when the walls of the Hanoi Citadel he was building kept collapsing by using his hooves to delineate an area the walls should be built instead.

According to a sign on the temple grounds, it was originally built on Long Do Mountain (we're not sure where that is these days) until it was moved to its current location, tucked into the centre of the Old Quarter, to act as the guard of the east of Thang Long in the 18th century during the Ly Dynasty. A statue of the temple's eponymous horse today stands beside the altar.

The temple has been repaired many times, the sign notes, and in 1839 a shrine to Confucius was added to the left of the temple, while a

Phoenix altar was constructed to make offerings to the seasons. The current structure is typical of Hanoi pagodas.

Bach Ma is still very actively used for worship note the extended hours on the 1st and 15th of each lunar month to accommodate those who regularly come with offerings to burn

Bach Ma Temple

76 Hang Buom, Hanoi

Tues-Sun 08:00-11:00, 14:00-17:00. 1st and 15th of the lunar month 08:00-21:00.

Ba Da Pagoda

Chua Ba Da is an historic pagoda tucked away down an alley just near St Joseph's Cathedral.

It's a touch difficult to find (we had to ask a security guard across the road to point it out), but look for the archway with "Chua Ba Da" written across the top on Nha Tho, the street leading down to St Jospeph's Cathedral. Wander down the alley and it opens into a wide, leafy courtyard, at the back of which lies a traditional-style temple building, still actively used by worshippers.

Legend has it that a pagoda was first built on the site during the 11th century when Emperor Ly Thanh Tong ruled. Later on, during construction work on the Thang Long Citadel during the 15th century, a stone statue of a woman was unearthed. The statue was brought here, and the temple was renamed Ba Da (stone lady). The statue has since disappeared, but the pagoda is still worth a peek for its lovely (and conveniently located) setting.

Ba Da Pagoda

Nha Tho St, Hanoi

Admission: Free

Museums

Hanoi Police Museum

While told from a clearly pro-government perspective, the Hanoi Police Museum showcases the interesting history of Hanoi's police force and offers some fascinating photographs and exhibits to explore.

Set in a thoughtfully laid out and spacious single-storey building, the museum has exhibits labelled clearly in Vietnamese, French and English, and takes the visitor through the chronological history of the police force in the Vietnamese capital.

The force was founded in 1946 out of the Tonkin Security Police. While they were still the Tonkin Security Police, the officers "were engaged in the fight against the traitors and the collaborators of the French and the Japanese in order to protect the party and the revolutionary movements and participate in the insurrection of 1945." The initial exhibits of photos, documents and weapons take the visitor through the police efforts to expel the French and "kill the traitors", from 1946 through to 1954.

The next room covers 1954-75 and the police fight against the CIA as Vietnam slides into war with the United States. Another room traverses 1975-86, when the capital expands dramatically and national and international forces conspire "to destroy the creation of socialism in Vietnam"; all is well, however, as the Hanoi police work hard to expose these networks.

Finally, 1986-2015 brings the police force up till today, more or less, when the focus tends to be on drugs, cyber crime, fake goods and even exam cheaters. Look for the wig on display that a cheater used!

On display are the uniforms of the police and their various departments over time, a motorbike or two and a few dioramas, such as an example of a police station in the 1990s. We followed our noses and walked into what we thought was an example of a realistic police office today... only to realise that it was actually a real office, not open to the public. Oops!

Ho Chi Minh Museum

The Ho Chi Minh Museum does exactly what, given its name, you would expect it to do. Opened in 1990 on the anniversary of Ho Chi Minh's birth, the Soviet-style museum is a bizarre hagiography brought to life.

After a visit to the man himself at the Ho Chi Minh Mausoleum, then a spin past the Presidential Palace and his two former homes, and a quick stop at the One Pillar Pagoda, an exploration of the Ho Chi Minh Museum is the next natural stop on a do-it-yourself Ho Chi Minh tour of Hanoi.

The first exhibits are primarily black and white photos, interspersed with books, letters, copies of speeches and the like. Captions are brief but informative, in English and Vietnamese, although there's a randomness about it all, as you'll find a black and white photo of the tank breaking down the gates at Independence Palace one pillar away from a colour photo of the first successful organ implant in Vietnam in 2004.

On the next floor, you'll be greeted by a massive statue of the man of the honour. It's awarded its own room, and what a room at that: high ceilings, tiled walls and intricate inlays abound.

Next up are a series of rather bizarre, 1970-style art installations that have the intention of depicting the world at the beginning of the 20th century in order to demonstrate the changes that were going on in the world that had a deep impact on "Ho Chi Minh's thinking and his quest for national liberation".

Themes covered include human hope and achievement versus the degradations of fascism, and you'll see Ho Chi Minh's hideout in Cao

Bang Cave rendered as a human brain. It's post-modernism influenced by pop art, with a heavy dose of socialist realism.

Vietnam Military History Museum

The Vietnam Military History Museum has a comprehensive collection of war relics charting Vietnam's struggle for liberation. If you're only going to see one war museum in Vietnam, this should be it. While the styles of the displays are definitely outdated by today's whizz-bang interactive exhibition standards, there is a lot of history packed into this museum that is still fascinating. The old museum style is in itself intriguing to observe.

There is a lot to see, so pace yourself, or decide what's really of interest to you. If you're mainly interested in the American War, you may want to skip through some of the earlier galleries, or risk being too overloaded with information to really appreciate it. Naturally everything is shown from the perspective of the Communist government.

The museum was opened in the 1950s, and still has the feel of something set up then. It contains some 150,000 artefacts, documents and photographs arranged in a series of galleries. Though much is somewhat stale, expect more than the usual collection of guns, spears and ammo (though these do feature heavily), with a good deal of photojournalism and historical background provided in English, French and Vietnamese. Items are not put fully into context, but if you have some knowledge of Vietnamese history, a lot will be interesting to see.

The museum begins with galleries featuring featuring axes and stone hoes dated as far back as 4,000 years ago; information notes that the state of Van Lang, the site of modern Vietnam, repelled outside invaders as early as 7th and 6th centuries BC. Now that's some wartime history to cover to bring us up to the present. Note the sly reference when Vietnam's land area is explained to it including the "Paracel Islands and Spratly Islands". There might be a few neighbouring nations who disagree.

Hoa Lo Prison (Hanoi Hilton)

Originally sprawling over 13 hectares, Hoa Lo Prison, better known as the Hanoi Hilton to Westerners in one of its later iterations, was one of the largest prisons built by the French in Indochina.

Opened in 1896 on the site of razed ceramics village Phu Khanh, the French simply called it Maison Centrale; Hanoi has grown around it to such an extent that it is now located near the town centre.

The prison's original purpose was to function as the end of the assembly line for the colonial system of jurisprudence, detaining Vietnamese criminals who were more often than not anti-colonial revolutionaries (otherwise known to the Vietnamese as 'revered heroes and martyrs'). It was the inmates who dubbed it Hoa Lo, which means 'fiery furnace'. Cell D, for instance, from 1930 to 1945, held up to 100 political prisoners in an area designed for 40.

Surviving Hoa Lo or better yet, escaping from it gave a Viet Minh cadre powerful credentials, and more than a few of those who did went on to become central figures in the Communist Party. The museum's curators focus primarily on this period of the prison's history, but after the French were ousted in 1954 it was used to incarcerate a new set of Vietnamese 'criminals': counter-revolutionaries opposed to the growing influence of the party.

Then, during the American War, yet another new group of 'liberators' or despicable imperialist bandits were detained in the form of downed American pilots. From 1964 to 1973, Hoa Lo served as a prisoner-of-war camp and once again received a new, unofficial name: the Hanoi Hilton. The Vietnamese maintain that American prisoners were well-treated, but published memoirs by former inmates speak of torture, murder, medical neglect, and being fed food contaminated with faeces. The treatment was so bad here that some observers still maintain it constitutes a war crime. The Hanoi Hilton name became so resonant in popular culture that when the Hilton Corporation finally opened a hotel in Hanoi 1999, they had to awkwardly name it the Hilton Hanoi Opera to avoid tapping into any dark

Vietnamese Women's Museum

The Vietnamese Women's Museum is one of the best museums in Hanoi and is well worth a visit for anyone interested in the culture of Vietnam. It gives insight into Vietnam's 54 ethnic groups, addressed through the lens of women's issues.

The museum, which features more than 1,000 objects and photographs, is well laid out and bright, with quality exhibits, and the content is extensive and well presented, with information in Vietnamese, English and French.

Specifically, the museum is dedicated to the research, collection and exhibition of the life stories and experiences of Vietnamese women. As one of the first exhibits notes, "Women have always played an important role in the defence of the Vietnamese nation. In AD40, the Trung Sisters led the battle for independence against the Han Chinese..." And so it goes on.

Exhibits are spread over five floors, accessible by elevator if required. On the ground floor you'll find bag storage and a gift shop, mostly selling the type of souvenirs you'll also find in Old Quarter. Audio tours are available, lasting for a couple of hours. We didn't do one, but if you have the time, we suspect it would be a very worthwhile experience.

When we last dropped by, a temporary photographic exhibition was on display in the forecourt of the museum, with beautiful portraits of

Vietnamese women taken by French photographer Rehahn. Temporary exhibitions are always showing, so fingers crossed something else lovely will be showing on your stop here, too.

The museum comprises three permanent thematic galleries: Women in Family, Women in History and Women's Fashion. The family exhibition on the first floor looks at the roles and responsibilities of women in the typical Vietnamese family, and looks at traditional marriage and childbirth customs across ethnic groups. Another exhibit looks at meal preparations and agricultural practice, as well as small business and handicrafts such as sewing and weaving .

Vietnam Museum of Ethnology

The Vietnam Museum of Ethnology is a little out of the way from Hanoi's main sights, but as one of the city's best and most informative museums, it's worth seeking out. If you're planning on going trekking to the north and northwest of Hanoi, this museum should really be considered essential, but it goes well beyond covering the groups who live there.

The museum is set in three distinct parts. An older indoor area focuses on Vietnam's various ethnic groups, while a significant portion of the museum behind this is spread across a lovely sprawling garden filled with well-crafted examples of traditional houses from ethnic minority groups. A rather spectacular newer building off to the right features an exquisite Southeast Asian handicraft collection, that as of mid-2017 was only partially complete, with several empty rooms, but is still worth exploring.

The older building features exhibits from the everyday lives of Vietnam's 54 ethnic groups: the Viet (Kinh) and 53 minority groups, who together speak languages spread across five linguistic families. Displays, labelled in English, French and Vietnamese throughout, are both comprehensive and fascinating, covering all the main minority groups. Plentiful audiovisual displays are offered along with more typical museum fare and dioramas. Some items on display are simply breathtaking.

Check out, for instance, Mr Pham Dang Uy's bicycle, loaded down with 800 wooden and bamboo fishtraps. There's a 1956-built Cham buffalo cart from Ninh Thuan province, which is able to pull two tonnes worth of goods; funerary statues from Gia Lai; a diorama of an initiation ceremony of the Red Yao in Yen Bai province, and another of Hmong weavers. We particularly liked the various windows from a Black Thai stilt house in Son La province, recreated from 1960s sketches and mounted on a wall of the museum.

Look out for the educational room where visitors can do various activities. When we stopped by, it was a simple stencil rubbing, aimed more at children than adults

Vietnam Museum of Ethnology

Nguyen Van Huyen St, Hanoi

Tues-Sun 08:30-17:30

T: (04) 3765 2193

Admission: 40,000 dong. Guide: 50,000 dong inside, 50,000 dong outside.

National Museum of Vietnamese History

The National Museum of Vietnamese History is spread across two sites; Site One is set in a stunning colonial-era building and houses some simply beautiful historically important exhibits, while Site Two (on Tran Quang Khai), which was formerly known as the Vietnam Museum of Revolution, is less compelling, but still worth a spin through.

The star of the two locations is Site One, which until a few years ago was what the National Museum of Vietnamese History referred to alone. Covering Vietnam's prehistory through to the Nguyen dynasty in 1945, it's set in a magnificent example of Indochinese architecture, which was until 1910 the French consulate and residence of the governor general.

The building was also home to the Ecole Francaise d'Extreme Orient (EFEO), during which time it became a museum to exhibit EFEO finds. Over time the building deteriorated, and it was not until the early

1930s, following a seven-year renovation, that what you can see now was realised. The entrance gives on to an impressive two-storey rotunda with exhibits all around and in many galleries to the rear.

As of 2017, the main permanent exhibition is 18 pieces dating from the seventh to 20th centuries and selected by Vietnam's prime minister to be "national treasures". They included bronze drums, Champa stellae, a Tran dynasty-era bell and Ho Chi Minh's prison diary; we particularly loved the "Statue of a panpipe-playing couple piggybacking", from the Dong Son era (circa 2,500 BC), and selected as a treasure in 2012.

Aside from the permanent exhibition, the ground floor traces Vietnam's ancient history, from the first Neolithic finds through to those of the 15th century. Some items date back as far as 10,000 BC and exhibits feature more than just the requisite pottery shards and axe heads.

The jewellery, tools and household items archaeologists have unearthed along with human and animal remains paint a compelling picture of the people who inhabited the region long ago, and provide a sense of how they are tied to Vietnam's modern inhabitants. (We loved the jewellery. Sometimes it's the little details that bring history home, like imagining a woman wearing a necklack 4,000 years ago that's not too far off what a woman might

National Museum of Vietnamese History

1 Trang Tien St and 216 Tran Quang Khai St, Hanoi

Daily 08:00-12:00, 13:30-17:30. Closed first Monday of the month.

T: (04) 3825 2853

banbientap@baotanglichsu.vn

Admission: 40,000 dong for access to both sites

Vietnam Fine Arts Museum

The Vietnam Fine Arts Museum has one of the best and most diverse art collections in the country, and a visit here will provide some good insight into Vietnamese culture and history.

The museum is set in a stunning three-storey, 1930s-era building, originally ordered built by the French to house the daughters of the colonial elite, who travelled from all over Indochina to Hanoi to study. After a renovation in the 1960s, during which some traditional architectural elements of Vietnamese communal houses were added, the museum was opened in 1966.

Some 3,000 permanent exhibits are on display, including sculptures, paintings and lacquerworks, arranged chronologically from bottom to top. While some information is provided in English, to get a real sense of the meaning of the works and how they relate to Vietnamese history, we'd advise either hiring a guide here though we didn't try one so can't say how good they might be or hopping on to one of Sophie's Art Tours. No audio guide is available.

Exhibits throughout are generally well-captioned. An attempt is made to put each room into a larger context, but the text is not always comprehensible and tends to spout the government's perspective you won't read how the government forced artists to switch from their French-, then Japanese-enforced styles to socialist realism.

Look closely too as some works are reproductions (and not very good ones at that). They may be labelled as such, but sometimes Vietnamese artists made several copies of their own work as was the Vietnamese way and it's not always clear even to experts today which ones are the original or the final works intended for display by the artist. Many artworks were also destroyed during the American War and some have not been maintained well enough

Vietnam Fine Arts Museum
66 Nguyen Thai Hoc St, Hanoi
Daily 08:30-17:00
T: (04) 3733 2131 F: (04) 3734 1427;
btmtvn@vnfam.vn
Admission: Adults/children: 40,000/20,000 dong. Guided tour: 150,000 dong.

The Ho Chi Minh Trail Museum

Located about 15km outside Hanoi, this is often a stop along the way to the Perfume Pagoda.

The two-storey museum has seven galleries dedicated to the system of trails collectively known as the Ho Chi Minh Trail.

The trail stretched from northern Vietnam along the Laos border at a latitude parallel to Vinh along the coast (which was the main port for supplies destined for the trail), down to Saigon in the south. Featuring clandestine spurs that slipped into neighbouring Laos and Cambodia, the trail led to no end of troubles for the United States, whose guidelines for making war prevented them from (legally) following the Viet Cong into those countries (though Special Forces often did anyway, and it's one of the reasons Nixon bombed Cambodia, an act which contributed greatly to his losing the war from a political standpoint). For the North Vietnamese, the trail is a testament to tenacity, engineering and just plain pluck in no small way it's why they won the war.

Displays are heavy on photojournalism from the period, and artefacts collected from along its length. There are some English captions, but not many. However, for war buffs and returning Vets, this museum has one of the best collections of captured American ordnance and military equipment in the country. It's almost as if the curators are trying to prove to the world that the Americans were there, on the trail, often where they shouldn't have been. There's a particularly evocative display of IDs, uniforms and personal possessions of American soldiers, which were supposedly found along the trail, including a GI helmet emblazoned with the slogan "Tiger Sharks Kill for Kicks," reminiscent of the Oliver Stone flick Full Metal Jacket.

On the second floor is a lecture hall featuring a dusty, poorly labelled diorama of the trail, but if you're familiar with the geography of Vietnam, it does give a good sense of the trail. Just outside the museum, transport vehicles and bulldozers from the period have been enshrined for posterity, a bit like in ancient times when elephants that died in battle were promoted to the rank of general and given their own elaborate tombs.

How to get there

To get here, head out of Hanoi southwest on Tay Son Road 14km to the turn off for the Perfume Pagoda (Route 21B in the town of Ba La) but keep going straight an additional kilometre. The sign is on the right pointing to the museum way back off the road it's in Vietnamese so look out for 'Bao Tang Duong Ho Chi Minh'.

It's also an easy journey by public transport: pick up the No 2 bus in town (it stops along Trang Thi, to the South West of Hoan Kiem lake, and Ton Duc Thang, which runs alongside the Temple of Literature) and stay on until the very last stop which is Yen Nghia bus station. Exit the bus station, turn left and then left again and the Museum's about 500m off the road.

The Ho Chi Minh Trail Museum

15km outside Hanoi

Tue-Sat 07:30 to 11:00 and 13:30 to 14:30

Admission: 10,000 dong

Public parks and zoos

Hoan Kiem Lake

A visit to Hanoi would be incomplete without a wander around Hoan Kiem Lake, the centrepiece of the city. No matter the time of day, the lake is surrounded by activity and points of interest.

Ho (lake) Hoan Kiem means "Lake of the Returned Sword". Legends as to how it acquired its current name vary in detail, but all relate to nationalist hero Emperor Le Loi, who borrowed a magic sword and used it to defeat aggressive Chinese forces before returning it to a turtle that surfaced in the lake. A giant turtle known as Cu Rua in fact lived in the lake for decades or longer before dying in January 2016, to the shock of many Vietnamese, who had considered the 160-kilogram beast sacred. The huge turtle had become a symbol of Vietnamese independence and resilience, and was one of the last four Yangtze giant soft-shell turtles left on earth.

A small shrine in the centre of the lake was built in the 1880s to honour the turtle; it can't be visited, but certainly makes the lake more photogenic. Now, we don't know whether there are any other turtles in the lake, but we swear we saw something rear its head and take a breath as we stood on the lake's shores just near the giant clock at the southern end of the lake.

A walk right around Hoan Kiem Lake is highly recommended. It's a great opportunity for people watching, you'll pass plenty of points of interest and, if you stick to the garden pathways, you won't have to navigate or cross Hanoi's infamous streets for a while.

Gardens line the banks of the lake and are stunning around spring and festival times, when lanterns and other decorations add to the already attractive scenes. The lake is a central gathering point on these special occasions. It's the place to go for New Year fireworks or the mid-autumn festival, as long as you can handle crowds. It's also a popular spot for wedding photographs and for young lovers, who take advantage of the many benches in the gardens to snuggle. During spring, potted flowers add riotous colour, and as Hanoi shakes off its winter gloom the cafes surrounding the lake take on a distinctly

Thong Nhat Park

Thong Nhat (or Reunification) Park is a great spot to relax with a book or enjoy a hassle-free stroll or jog. While you wouldn't come out of your way to visit as a tourist, if you're looking to do a spot of people-watching or running, it will do the trick very nicely.

The park covers an area of more than 50 hectares in Hai Ba Trung district, to the south of Hoan Kiem. It was inaugurated in 1960, at which time the country was divided; the park was named Thong Nhat which means 'united', expressing the hope of reunification. In 1980, on the 110th anniversary of Lenin's birth, the name was changed to Lenin Park, but it was changed back to Thong Nhat. (Lenin Park is now the name of a small park on Dien Bien Phu, opposite the Vietnam Military History Museum and Flag Tower).

Thong Nhat is spacious, with a variety of trees spread across well-manicured lawns. Plenty of pathways let you jog or walk, with a circuit around the seven-hectare lake, Bay Mau, in the centre of the park making a good goal. Benches are on offer for a spot of reading or relaxing and there are toilets. While you can expect to receive smiles and hellos you are unlikely to be approached by anyone trying to sell you something or ask for donations, a pleasant break compared to Old Quarter.

A bridge on one bank leads to a picture-perfect island and the columns set up to the north of the lake we assume for wedding photography may feel out of sorts in Hanoi but contribute to the prettiness of the park.

Various events are held at the park, such as Lunar New Year fireworks, and we just missed out on seeing a Bulgarian rose festival, of all things.

We did get to see some interesting animal topiary though, apparently done to celebrate the start of the year of the rooster.

Kids' rides scattered throughout the park can best be described as rickety and rusty. When we last visited on a weekday they were shuttered, and though they seemed to be past their prime it looked like they may well operate over the weekends when more families visit.

West Lake

Also known as Ho Tay or Lake of Mist, West Lake covers a sizeable part of northwest Hanoi and offers an array of attractions.

While tourists flock to Old Quarter, West Lake is probably the most popular neighbourhood for expats. And while you'll find an abundance of Western-orientated restaurants, bars and shops here, normal and colourful Vietnamese life filters through all around them, from streetside food joints to fishermen and temples.

As well as escaping the busy streets of Hanoi, the lake provides an opportunity to watch fishermen at work, to see some very pretty temples scattered around the shore and to enjoy a coffee or beer while enjoying the breeze that comes across the lake (not so good on a cold and windy day, but lovely in summer). And the views across the lake on a sunny day are impressive.

According to legend, the lake was formed by the footprint of a golden calf running towards the sound of a giant bell. In its heyday, the lake was lined by royal palaces, which are now mostly gone and replaced by high-end housing and luxury hotels.

It's a 15-kilometre walk around the lake. Consider hiring a bicycle to circumnavigate the whole way clockwise so avoiding the need to cross over too many roads or do some of it on foot. Exploring a little, especially around the Sheraton and Intercontinental neighbourhoods, will have you stumble across cafes as well as streetside restaurants, and you'll see fishermen either patiently waiting for a catch, or in the lake itself.

Art galleries or venues

Mosaic wall

Hanoi is home to the world's largest mosaic mural wall, which snakes just shy of four kilometres along the Red River dyke running north to south to the east of city's Old Quarter.

The mosaic wall was unveiled to mark the thousand-year anniversary of the establishment of Hanoi, which was originally known as Thang Long and founded by Emperor Ly Thai To, in 2010.

The concept was developed by Vietnamese journalist and artist Nguyen Thu Thuy, who wanted to create a piece of public art along the 800-year-old graffiti- and advertisement-ridden wall in order to bring local communities within Hanoi together. Several dozen Vietnamese and international artists along with hundreds of children, were involved in the wall's design and construction, which started in 2007.

Every 100 metres or so a new design features on the wall: You'll notice decorative patterns from different Vietnamese historical periods along with more modern artworks and children's drawings. A smattering of recognisable world monuments, such as Indonesia's Borobodur, also appear. Various companies, embassies and other organisations, like the Goethe-Institut and the British Council, sponsor some sections of the wall,

The tiles measuring three by three centimetres were created by local artisans, many in Hanoi's Bat Trang ceramic village. Each square metre contains around a thousand tiles.

This is the largest ceramic mosaic in the world by area and is officially recognised as such by the Guinness Book of Records. It really is quite something, its colourful swirls brightening up an otherwise drab arterial road.

We wouldn't usually recommend spending any time on the dyke road but the mural is worth keeping an eye out for, even if it's just from a taxi en route to West Lake. In fact, viewing from a taxi or xe om is probably the best way to see it. The road changes name numerous times along its length but the section covered by the mosaic includes Tran Nhat Duat, Yen Phu

How to get there

From Old Quarter, walk along Luong Ngoc Quyen out towards Tran Nhat Duat. Directly opposite the end of Luong Ngoc Quyen you will see a large mural recognising Hanoi's 1,000-year anniversary. The mural runs to the left and right of this you'll need to walk a couple of hundred metres either way to get past the road junction to the mural.

Mosaic wall

Dyke Road, Hanoi

Admission: Free

Art galleries

Hanoi offers an array of art galleries, from commercial ones pumping out appealing art and copies for the masses through to higher-end spaces, where you might pick up an original $5,000 piece from one of Vietnam's in-demand artists.

Lovely independent contemporary art centre Manzi, set in a colonial-era two-storey building, has a small but carefully curated collection of works by emerging artists upstairs, and a relaxed cafe/bar downstairs. When we last passed through they were showing a beautiful temporary exhibition of works by 1986-born Vo Tran Chau, the highlight of which was a long con, or an emperor's ritual garment, sewed together from pieces of fabric handed down by her ancestors.

Founded by Suzanne Lecht in Hanoi in 2002, Art Vietnam is open by appointment only. It presents emerging and well established Vietnamese and foreign artists and while we haven't yet checked it out, Suzanne is extremely well regarded in Vietnam's art circles and would be an important contact for anyone interested in more serious pieces. Art Vietnam's website gives you a good idea of the kinds of work Vietnamese artists are producing and what you can expect to see.

It's no longer an official gallery, but you might find the door open at Salon Natasha, the Old Quarter home of Russian art expert and dealer Natasha Kraevskaia, who was married to the late provocative avant garde artist Vu Dan Tan. The shopfront remains scattered with artworks, and Natasha is passionate about Vietnamese art.

Sumptuous Apricot Gallery offers commercially popular art downstairs, and as you head upstairs floor after floor the collection become more expensive; this is one of Hanoi's more extensive art galleries. You could easily lose an hour or two here immersed in the stunning

Markets
Quang Ba Flower Market

If you love flowers, you'll love a poke around Hanoi's colourful and photogenic Quang Ba Flower Market, where masses of glorious flowers are bought and sold by the impossibly laden-motorbike-full.

Primarily a wholesale market, vendors buy from pick-up trucks bringing in flowers and greenery from Da Lat and Hanoi's outer suburbs, and on-sell to buyers from retail shops and the bicycle vendors you'll see roving across town. If you just can't resist, they will still sell retail to individual buyers.

This is Hanoi's busiest flower market, and it's supposed to really get going from around 02:00 till 06:00, but we dropped by around midnight and it was still interesting to see. You'll genuinely be amazed at the volume of flowers being packed onto single motorbikes. We spied sunflowers, roses, chrysanthemums, orchids, gerberas, lilies, hydrangeas and various kinds of greenery being sold at the market. A couple of stalls sell arrangements, but mostly the same kind of flower is sold by the bundle. The single globes used to illuminate the market add to the atmosphere.

As with any busy market, keep your eyes peeled for motorbikes zipping along unexpected spaces, and be ready to get out of the way.

The market is a way out of the Old Quarter in Tay Ho, but if you like flowers it's definitely worth the trip. Keep a visit to the market in mind particularly if you're arriving in Hanoi on the overnight train from

Sapa, which gets in at around 05:00, as dropping by will let you kill a little time till the rest of the city

Quang Ba Flower Market

Off Au Co, Tay Ho, Hanoi

Best 00:00-6:00.

Admission: Free

Chau Long Market

Chau Long Market is a great example of an everyday Hanoi wet market. Come early for the full experience, or a little later in the morning for a more relaxed wander.

Chau Long is a traditional wet market, selling predominantly (very) fresh meat, fish and vegetables. Despite the growth of supermarkets, most Vietnamese still do the bulk of their shopping at wet markets, either at covered places like Chau Long, or less permanent streetside set-ups.

The environment is dark and wet, and you will need to keep your eyes peeled to dodge the motorbikes zipping along the narrow aisles, but it's also atmospheric, eye-opening and educational. In one tucked away corner you'll find a few workers cleaning and prepping frogs, day in, day out. You'll find freshly plucked chooks and ducks, an array of seafood, and all kinds of meat cuts, along with colourful fruit and veggies. Stalls brim with groceries such as noodles rice, oils and sauces as well.

Although you may arouse some interest, the stallholders here are used to foreigners: Hanoi Cooking Centre is just up the road and Chau Long is the market they visit at the start of a cooking class or street food tour, plus it's a popular spot with expats.

You'll also find a parade of similar stalls outside on Chau Long Street, along with a shop grinding grains. Walk further around the market and you'll come across some food stalls, selling the usual array of street food dishes like com binh dan and bun cha.

Similar markets include Cho Hom on Pho Hue, which is a bit larger and more spread out, and Yen Phu market

Chau Long Market
Between Chau Long/Tran Vu, Truc Bach
Admission: Free

Long Bien Market

It's not top of any must-do list in travel guides, but a visit to Hanoi's chaotic Long Bien market is a fascinating exposure to the life of a large proportion of Hanoi residents. But you'll need to get up early very early.

Long Bien market, located next to Long Bien bridge, alongside the dyke road, is a fruit and vegetable wholesale market and is at its busiest in the very early hours of the morning, when stallholders from the local wet markets, restaurants and other businesses visit to stock up for the day. Fruit and vegetables come in from the Vietnamese countryside and from China, arriving in trucks from around 01:00. A drive or walk along Yen Phu the main road at any time between 01:00 and 06:00 will give you an insight into the life of the market, but to experience it in all its glory you'll need to head on inside.

You may have visited a wet market in Vietnam before but Long Bien market is on a completely different level. At its peak, around 03:00, it is a heaving mass of activity: buyers crowd around open-back trucks, vying for a bargain; money counters hold court over their stalls, recording every sale; motorbikes weave down aisles, loaded with boxes and bags crammed with fruit; workers squat in front of huge baskets of fruit, sorting the good from the bad; and paths are blocked by carts competing with bicycles and shoppers, with neither willing to give way.

Being a night market also gives it a different vibe: vendors operate under fluorescent strip lights or single bulbs, bringing a eerie glow to the multitude of alleyways created by canvas and wooden makeshift dividers. As the sun comes up, the lights go off and daylight replaces artificial lighting. By 06:00, shoppers are replaced by a plethora of street cleaners, sweeping up the crushed packing material and squashed oranges, and vendors take a break for breakfast and to count the day's takings.

Everywhere you look there is a treat for the senses at Long Bien. So visit, walk around, and find a spot to just watch the time flies by.

As a final note, and without wishing to put a dampener on things, the market does have a darker side. Many of the workers, particularly the porters, have emigrated from surrounding rural areas to earn money to send home to poor families. For women, this means leaving children behind and relocating to a cramped, damp room, shared with others in the same situation. Pay is low, the work is hard and abuse is common.

A recent exhibition at the Women's Museum "Shining Night" relayed the lives of migrant women (and men) working in Long Bien market through displays and personal stories. It's no longer on display.

Dong Xuan market

Hanoi's oldest market Dong Xuan mainly sells bulk food items, clothing and accessories targeted towards locals in its three storeys of packed aisles.

The original market opened in 1889, and while the facade remains, the interior was completely rebuilt after a fire in 1994 that killed several people.

Dong Xuan takes up an entire city block. It's huge and really does sell pretty much everything, though it's not really a tourist market. If you're looking for gifts to take home then you're better off hunting around Hang Gai and Hang Hom. A few stalls do sell the usual tourist paraphernalia silk cushion covers, chopsticks so it won't be a wasted trip if that's what you're after, but don't go expecting a wealth of options.

Come though simply to experience a typical Southeast Asian wet market on the ground floor and in the market's surrounds, where you'll see plenty of colourful fresh produce as well as sacks full of dried mushrooms, fish and other dry goods. Upstairs is mainly cloth and clothes, and there's a food hall here too, though the ones just outside the market seem to attract more of a crowd, at least during the day (perhaps it's busy early morning). Shops surround the streets leading onto the market; we snapped up some coffee filters at one of the shops just outside the market for 20,000 dong each.

Don't go during lunch or in the early afternoon, when it's siesta time. Unless you want to have to nudge the stallholders from their slumber or interrupt their lunch, which is not likely to get you a good price, come earlier in the day or late in the afternoon. Do be careful of your belongings, too. There have been reports of theft and it's easy to see why: the aisles are narrow and there's a lot of squeezing through gaps, when it's easy for someone to reach into an open bag or slit it open.

How to get there

To get there head up Hang Ngang Street from the junction of Hang Bo/Hang Bac and keep going straight. You can't miss the market.

Dong Xuan market

Bordered by Nguyen Thien Thuat, Cao Thang, Hang Khoai and Tran Nhat Duat, Hanoi

General activities

Gyms

For most people a holiday is a chance to escape from the gym well, it certainly used to be for me but for longer-term visitors who want to work off the bia hoi, or gym addicts, Hanoi offers a selection of gyms, both cheap and pricey.

Aside from exercising in the park, the cheapest options are the local gyms. For the equivalent of just a dollar or two entrance fee you can use basic equipment in a somewhat grubby testosterone-fuelled environment. Club Olympia is the most popular place for non-locals, by all accounts, and is located on Tran Hung Dao Street, south of Hoan Kiem. It has both weights and CV equipment and I've heard it also runs aerobics classes.

Or head to Gym Club G on Xuan Dieu it's a measly 20,000 VND but only has a poor range of free weights and a few weights machines. Still, it does the job if you just want to build up those pecs. There's another branch in Cau Giay which gets better reviews, but it's quite a trek.

Unfortunately, gyms in Hanoi are either dirt cheap or ridiculously expensive: so to the expensive...

NShape Fitness, towards the Daewoo Hotel, is very well rated: it's small, with just one studio for classes, but has high-quality equipment and a decent changing room with sauna and steam room, and is cool and immaculately clean. A six-month membership is $100 per month, with no joining fee, or buy a day pass for $17. Price includes use of all facilities.

Elite Fitness, on Xuan Dieu, is the new kid on the block. Its high end facilities extend to a swimming pool and spa but at a price: 22m VND ($1,100) for six months and 600,000VND ($30) for a day pass. Look out for promotions on longer term memberships.

Alternatively try the hotels: most top end places offer daily membership of their fitness centres. For example, the Daewoo charges $25 and Fortuna Hotel is $21, both including use of the spa and swimming pool a better deal than the gyms.

Club Olympia

4 Tran Hung Dao, Hanoi

T: (04) 3933 1049

Gym Club G

Alley 31, Xuan Dieu, Tay Ho, Hanoi

NShape Fitness

5th floor, Vuon Xuan building, 71 Nguyen Chi Thanh Street, Dong Da, Hanoi

T: (04) 6266 0495 / (0912) 348 555

sales@nshapefitness.vn

Elite Fitness

51 Xuân Di?u, Tây H?, Hanoi (next to Syrena Towers)
T: (04) 3718 6281
E: info@elitefitness.com.vn

Daewoo Hotel

360 Kim Ma Street, Ba Dinh District, Hanoi
T: (04) 3831 5555
E: reservation@daewoohotel.com.vn

Fortuna Hotel

6B Lang Ha Street, Ba Dinh, Hanoi
T: (04) 3831 3333
E: fortunahanoi@fortunahotel.com.vn

Lacquerware classes

Lacquer items paintings, photo albums, bowls, vases are a popular souvenir in Vietnam. Old Quarter in Hanoi is flooded with shops selling the same selection of items at the same negotiable prices. But why not make your own take-home piece of lacquerware? Here's how.

We checked out the Lacquer Art Tay Ho studio in Tay Ho district where classes are taught by Tran Anh Tuan, a professor at the Fine Arts' Institute and a lacquer specialist. After just one lesson we realised how much work goes into the paintings and wondered how the piles of paintings for sale in Old Quarter could be sold so cheaply.

What we discovered is that most paintings on sale are made in a factory and use Japanese or industrial paint rather than traditional lacquer as these dry faster so speed up the process. They also do the arduous and time-consuming grinding and polishing by machine, rather than by hand. So mass production, machine processes and lower cost materials contribute to the low price items you'll find in most shops. So if you want the real thing, made in the traditional way, you'll need to look further afield and be prepared to pay hundreds, if not thousands, of dollars.

But back to the classes. Classes can be paid for in blocks or as you go, so we initially just went along for one class to see what it was all about. Students can join at any time and attend as little or often as suits, so it's not so much a class as a workshop, where everyone gets on with their own piece with help and advice from Tuan as required.

First we were given a quick introduction to the different techniques by Tuan's assistant Tuan's English isn't great, although he gets by. The main techniques used are eggshell, mother of pearl and silver leaf, and paints are either transparent or solid.

I was instructed to get a board and draw my picture. That was something I hadn't given any thought to so after a bit of head scratching and an attempt to draw a chilli I opted for a fried egg.

If you're only in Hanoi short-term you can still have a go. It's feasible to complete a simple picture in one lesson, but if you can squeeze a few in you'll get more out of it the egg painting took me around five sessions, but I took my time.

The Lacquer Art Tay Ho studio is located in Tay Ho District, behind the large Sedona Suites building on Xuan Dieu. Classes run for 2.5 hours during various morning, afternoon and evening slots.

What to do with kids in Hanoi

The crazy streets and hectic traffic in Hanoi make it seem less than child-friendly, but the city offers many activities that children will enjoy. Here's a selection of things to do with kids in the Vietnamese capital.

Most people want to explore Hanoi's atmospheric Old Quarter with its famed 36 streets, but walking around the area with young children can be stressful as you negotiate your way around streetside barbecues, speeding (and parked) motorbikes plus shop displays spilling onto the road. Avoid the stress by taking an hour-long ride on one of Hanoi's electric cars, which cost 300,000 dong for an hour-long tour. The cars seat up to seven adults officially, or probably five or six Westerners comfortably. Head to the north end of Hoan Kiem lake, and you can't miss the cluster of them parked there with a ticket booth. You can also ask your hotel to arrange for them to pick you up directly. Do this early on during your stay as it will help you get your bearings of the city. Another more traditional option is to hire a cyclo (or two) to guide you round the city. An hour is plenty to get an initial taste of Hanoi and a few key sights.

If you do want to walk to explore, then avoid the central part of Old Quarter and spend your time to the east, along roads like Hang Vai and Hang Ga, or near St Joseph's Cathedral, where streets are quieter and, in the cathedral area at least, the shopping is good, too. A large number of Western-oriented cafes are also in this area we liked colourful Eden, in particular. If the traffic doesn't bother you, kids will love Old Quarter's Luong Van Can Toy Street

Lotus flowers

When lotus flower season hits in June, the West Lake area becomes awash with the blooms, which hold particular significance in Vietnam, where they are considered one of four graceful plants, along with pine, bamboo and chrysanthemum.

They are a symbol of purity, commitment, optimism for the future, beauty, majesty, grace, fertility, wealth, richness, knowledge, serenity... anything positive really. A famous Vietnamese song, "Doa hoa vo thuong", is about the lotus flower

Such is the Vietnamese love for the lotus that it was voted as the country's national flower for which one of the criteria was that it "must be found in many localities", and inded it would be hard to travel through Vietnam during lotus season without coming across a pond or lake filled with them.

There are four large ponds around the banks of West Lake filled with lotus flowers. One is near the waterpark and the other three are along the northern bank. If you take a bike ride around the lake you can't miss them.

Early in the morning, elderly ladies push off in their boats to cut the flowers ready for selling later that day. Later in the day, young lovers and groups of girls dressed up in ao dai scoot along to the ponds for both professional and amateur photo shoots. Enterprising land or pond owners have put up bridges jutting out into the ponds and charge for the privilege of taking photos on the bridge or out on small boats among the flowers.

The white and pink flowers are most commonly seen in the ponds and streets of Hanoi, with pink being considered the supreme of all lotuses.

Flower vendors can be found selling bunches, wrapped in a lotus leaf, from bicycles all around the city, particular at the western end of Pho Yen Phu, which makes for a wonderful photo opportunity. They're not too expensive, at around 30,000 VND a bunch, but they die very soon after the bloom. You will also see the dried seed heads for sale; they resemble the spouts of watering cans and make a contemporary addition to flower displays.

As well as being beautiful to look at, and having a wonderful fragrance, lotus flowers have other uses: the young stems are used in salads, the stamens can be dried and made into a herbal tea and the lotus seeds are eaten raw, dried or boiled. The sweet soup is particularly tasty.

Churches
Cua Bac
Cua Bac Church was built in 1932 by the French and is one of the most important in Hanoi today for Catholics.

Originally called Church of the Martyrs, the 700-capacity church was designed in a somewhat eclectic style by French architect Ernest Hebrard, featuring a bell tower on one side of the main building and various Art Deco touches though the roof tiles remain in Vietnamese style.

In November 2006, US President George W. Bush attended a joint worship service here among Vietnamese Catholics and Protestants, saying afterwards that: "A whole society is a society which welcomes basic freedom, and there's no more basic freedom than the freedom to worship..." President Bush's visit came as the United States had hailed the government for its improvements in advancing religious freedom.

The church was renovated in 2014, when it was given a fresh coat of ochre paint, wiping away something of its erstwhile crumbling charm. Aesthetics aside, along with St Joseph's Cathedral, Cua Bac is one of the most important for Catholics in the city.

Today the church's name of Cua Bac is taken due to its proximity to the Thang Long Citadel's Northern Gate (Cua Bac); while you might not seek this church out unless you're attending a service, you can pop your head in if you're visiting the citadel without going out of your way.

St Joseph's Cathedral

The beautiful neo-Gothic St Joseph's Cathedral in downtown Hanoi was consecrated in 1886 and remains active today thanks to the city being home to a large community of local Catholics.

Vietnam is predominantly Buddhist, but that didn't stop the French colonists from attempting to save souls the Catholic way. The French demolished 800-year-old Bao Thien pagoda, which stood on the site and was important to the Vietnamese, in order to build the distinctly European-style church. It was built by French missionary and apostolic vicar of Tonkin Paul-François Puginier, with Paris' Notre Dame in mind. The still very active bell towers reach 31.5 metres high, making this an impressive building.

The church was closed in 1975 upon the reunification of Vietnam, and was not reopened until 1985; mass was only held again in 1990.

Access the cathedral via a side door, as the frontage is blocked off by temporary gating. The interior is majestic, and the church is known for its beautiful, French-produced stained glass incredibly, the original has survived decades of tumultuous times.

The square around the cathedral is popular with locals just hanging out sipping tea and munching on sunflower seeds along the footpaths, and during the spring wedding season you'll likely see couples having pre-wedding photos taken outside the church.

We suggest heading to the rooftop of Eden to enjoy the view with a coffee, or the balcony of Hanoi House to sip a beer and watch the goings on in the square. For a meal, try La Place or Marilyn, both with balconies looking on to

St Joseph's Cathedral
40 Nha Chung, Hoan Kiem, Hanoi
Mon-Sat 08:00–11:00, 14:00-17:00. Sun 07:00-11:30, 15:00-21:00.
Admission: Free

Hiking, walking tours and itineraries

One day in Hanoi

Hanoi is often, sadly, just somewhere visitors stop off for a night or two en route to Ha Long Bay, mountainous Sapa or a dash down the coast to Ho Chi Minh City. But for those who do want to take a look around, however fleeting, Hanoi can be a fascinating destination in its own right. So, if you just have one day in Hanoi, how do you make the most of it?

Before you jump in with an "everyone's different" comment yes, I know, and if you like I'll write a dozen of these, but just for fun, here's how I would spend just one, very long, day in Hanoi... on something of a budget.

On an ideal day I'd be full of energy and would jump up out of bed before 6am to go and watch the early morning exercisers around Hoan Kiem Lake. Not to participate you understand, just to observe.

The early start would certainly deserve a fine breakfast reward and for that I'd wander to Puku just because I love Eggs Benedict and they do a decent one. It's a 10 - 15 minute walk from the lake, but as good a time as any to experience the atmosphere of Old Quarter and "Food Street", where Puku is now located, is usually quite lively.

After breakfast I'd take a slow walk along Phung Hung where there's a small market and down Bat Dan into the heart of Old Quarter to pick up a cyclo. Walking around Old Quarter is a good way to explore but if I just want to look around and take photos a cyclo makes life easier even if I do look a package holiday tourist. So I'd get a cyclo to take me around Old Quarter for a bit and then on to Tran Quoc Pagoda on West Lake.

The temple itself is worth a wander and the walk along Thanh Nien street between the two lakes always fills me with pleasure. Quan Thanh Temple, at the southern end of the street, has been refurbished recently, so I'd pop in there for a look around and then walk across to the small park opposite and find somewhere to sit and enjoy an iced or hot tea weather dependent and watch the world go by.

Fluids restored I'd take a five minute walk to the Botanical Gardens and walk through to the back entrance of the Ho Chi Minh Museum. I really like the area around the Museum and Mausoleum, it has a completely different feel to it to the rest of Hanoi. Maybe it's just the open spaces or the neatness of it all. If I were in the mood I'd visit the museum and I'd certainly go to see the stilt house where Ho Chi Minh lived for a while it provides an interesting insight to his life and is set in calming surroundings, a world away from the streets of Hanoi.

Then I'd jump on a xe om or in a taxi and head to the Temple of Literature. To be honest, it's a bit of a tourist trap and tends to be too busy to be able to really absorb its beauty and atmosphere, but it's still one of the most interesting places in Hanoi.

Koto a restaurant that trains disadvantaged youth is next to the Temple of Literature and is a good lunch spot, although I'd be tempted to find a *Bun Cha* stall instead as it's a must try in Hanoi.

After lunch I'd head back to Hoan Kiem and wander from the Opera House, past the Sofitel Metropole Legend and along Ngo Quyen to absorb the beautiful architecture of that part of the French Quarter. Then round the bottom of the lake and onto Le Thai To for dessert: Fanny's ice cream is to die for, but on a hot day I'd be tempted to sit at Hapro Bon Mua opposite for outdoor seating and a view of the lake.

By now it must be time for a bit of shopping and it's easy enough to walk from the lake to Hang Trong, Hang Gai, Hang Manh and Hang Hom where there are a high concentration of souvenir, clothes and art shops. Tan My Design, at 61 Hang Gai, is a particularly lovely shop to wander around, though it's a bit pricey for my budget.

After all that walking a massage is in order. Depending upon where I end up with my shopping I might go down to St Josephs Cathedral and try one of the places there, or will head to Dinh Liet to Emperor Foot Massage or Placencare for something a bit fancier.

After freshening up for the evening I'd aim to be at Avalon for sundowners the view's great and although it's not cheap it's worth it for one. But if money were tight I'd join the tourist hoards at International Bia Hoi corner for 4,000VND glasses of beer and a more down to earth literally view of life.

Dinner is where it gets tricky. There are so many options. I'm a big fan of griddled beef and so if I'm in the mood for that I'd head to 47 Ma May, but sitting on a plastic stool isn't always my bag so I'd either go to Gecko, on Luong Ngoc Quyen, for convenience, Little Hanoi on Ta Hien for cheapy Vietnamese or Green Tangerine if I wanted to splash out a bit.

For after dinner drinks, if I'm not out for a late one, Nolas on Ma May is a pleasant place to enjoy a cocktail or glass of wine and have a good natter. If I want a bit more atmosphere then I like Le Pub on Hang Be certainly not classy but usually busy and the outside area's great if you can get a seat. Then it's home in a taxi. Tired, a little bit inebriated and ready to head to Ha Long Bay.

Two days on a budget in Hanoi

Most people travelling through Hanoi give the city a couple of days before heading to Halong Bay, Sapa or down to the centre and south of the country. Here are our suggestions for what to do on a tight budget if you have just two days here and want to make the most of them.

On day one, explore Old Quarter. This is one of Hanoi's highlights and could take up the best part of a day especially if you're really into souvenir shopping or take lots of breaks to enjoy the delicious local coffee or street snacks. If you're on foot, this is free although you'll have to pay for refreshments and souvenirs.

Make sure you include a stop at Bach Ma Temple on Hang Buom Street, wander along Hang Ma and Lan Ong Streets and do check out the stalls around the outskirts of Dong Xuan, the market along Phung Hung, shopping around Hang Giay, St Joseph's Cathedral and of course Hoan Kiem Lake.

Then take a detour from the south of Hoan Kiem Lake for a peek at the Opera House and Sofitel Metropole Hotel, in the French Quarter.

If your budget stretches this far, negotiate with a cycle driver for a tour around Old Quarter and the French Quarter it'll save your legs and is a unique (albeit very touristy) experience.

End day one, or start day two, with a visit to a wet market. Take a taxi or xe om (motorbike taxi) or you can walk from the Old Quarter to Hom market (Cho Hom) on Pho Hue or Chau Long market, near Truc Bach lake. Go early in the morning or towards the end of the afternoon, when the markets are most lively.

Spend the rest of day two checking out a few museums or landmarks, which are usually cheap to see in Hanoi. Our favourites are the Women's Museum, Hoa Lo Prison, the National Fine Arts Museum, the Citadel and the Ethnology Museum; take your pick depending on your preferences. Note that the latter is a bit out of town, so if you're tight on time it might not be feasible, especially if you're travelling by bus (No 14, just in case).

And no visit to Hanoi is complete without a visit to the Ho Chi Minh Memorial Complex. Head there first thing if you want to see Ho Chi Minh's body, as it's only open in the morning and it's best to get there early to avoid queuing in the heat for too long, and don't miss the house on stilts. From here, walk up to Quanh Thanh Temple and along between Truc Bach and West Lakes to Tran Quoc Pagoda. Stop for an ice cream cone from Kem Tay Ho or head to Havana, overlooking the lakes, for a rooftop beer or cocktail. The Temple of Literature is another highlight, and walkable from the Mausoleum. You'll find a good bun cha joint nearby on Van Mieu, so stop off for lunch.

If you prefer the great outdoors to museum visits, rent a bicycle and cycle along the Red River or around West Lake.

As you go, eat, eat and eat. The street food in Hanoi is reasonably cheap and delicious, so with only two days in the city we say eat it for breakfast, lunch and dinner.

Four days in Hanoi

We've written about how we'd spend two days on a budget in Hanoi, but what about if you have a little longer? Linger for four days to see a bit more of Vietnam's capital, and here's what we'd suggest you do.

Take some tips from two days on a budget in Hanoi, but take your time: walk everywhere, visit more than one museum, stop for bia hoi or ice cream more regularly, hire a bicycle. Also consider incorporating some other free activities into your schedule, such as visiting Thong Nhat Park where you can easily while away half a day wandering around the lake, taking out a swan boat or sitting in the shade enjoying a beer or walking around Truc Bach Lake and its surrounds or the perimeter of West Lake.

Even if budget isn't so much of a consideration, we'd still recommend the suggestions from our two days in Hanoi post and above: in reality, a lot of the good stuff in Hanoi is free or cheap, and you certainly shouldn't miss out on exploring Old Quarter on foot, trying out the street food, visiting the museums, or people-watching from a cafe.

But to enhance your time consider taking a guided tour with a professional guide someone who can add to the visit experience with their knowledge and expertise. Either opt for a walking tour around Old Quarter, or take a guided tour of one of the museums. Check out Hidden Hanoi or Friends of Vietnam Heritage, contact the museum you're interested in directly or speak to a reputable travel agent. For the Museum of Ethnology or Museum of History, try contacting 54 Traditions Gallery: Mark Rapoport, one of the founders, provides excellent tours of both museums. Make sure to also check out his gallery if you're interested in ethnic minorities.

Fill half a day with a street food tour or a cooking course. Or both. For the latter, check out Hanoi Cooking Centre and read our reviews of street food tours for recommendations. Or read about what to do if you want to stay another day for some less usual Hanoi options: ice skating, cycling, paintballing or a photography tour perhaps? We would also schedule in some spa time, even if it's just a massage.

During the evenings, visit the night market, give the water puppets a go, look out for events at L'Espace and the Opera House and enjoy the social side of the city, whether it be *bia hoi* on the street, or a cocktail at Avalon.

If we were designing the four days, they would go something like this: day one in Old Quarter, with visits to the Women's Museum and Hoa Lu Prison; day two at the Ho Chi Minh Mausoleum Complex, with a walk across Duong Thanh Nien, incorporating Quanh Thanh Temple and Tran Quoc Pagoda and around Truc Bach Lake; day three on a bicycle ride to the surrounding countryside; and day four on a street food or cooking tour. And plenty of relaxing with beer, coffee or massage.

Hanoi on a splurge

We've covered Hanoi on a tight budget, but what if you've got a few extra dong to rub together during your visit to the Vietnamese capital? If you want to mix some luxury in with your Hanoi exploring, here are some suggestions.

Firstly, you'll want to check in somewhere beautiful. We have two favourite five-star hotels in Hanoi: the Sofitel Metropole Legend, which wins hands down for luxury, and the Intercontinental West Lake, a fabulous hotel as well in a winning location, with its pagodas projecting elegantly out into the lake and the charming Sunset Bar just ripe for a sundowner or three, it makes a great choice for a splurge.

For easy shopping, try Tan My Design on Hang Gai, where high-end versions of the souvenirs you'll find elsewhere along with a range of other items are available in an air-conditioned, peaceful environment.

If you want to splurge on original art, then try the shops on Hang Gai near Tan My Designs, or along Trang Tien. And the designer shops in the Sofitel Metropole, near the Opera House and in the new Trang Tien Plaza are a luxury shopaholic's dream.

A motorbike taxi or cyclo tour of Hanoi may not float your flash boat, so why not hire a classic car? The Sofitel Metropole hires out a classic Citroen car with driver for 2.2 million VND per hour. Take a bottle of champers along with you for a really romantic (and yes, pricey) experience.

For the perfect combination of adventure and a treat, we'd highly recommend going on a half-day street food tour with Hanoi Street Food Tours. True, sitting on plastic stools is not very luxurious, but the food's sensational and it's all an absolute feast for the senses.

Still on the food theme almost every five-star hotel in Hanoi does a buffet brunch at the weekend. The priciest option is the Sofitel Metropole's Sunday brunch at 1.5 million VND ++, which gets you all the steak, salmon, oysters and caviar you can eat, followed up by cheeses and a dessert platter. Throw in free-flow wine or champagne for an extra million or so. Or check out less pricey options at the Hanoi Hilton Opera or Movenpick Hotels.

Enjoying a cocktail with a lake view should be on your itinerary as well. We'd recommend either the rooftop of the Sofitel Plaza surely the best view in Hanoi or the Sunset Bar at the Intercontinental, where you can lounge on a bed while sipping a mojito and watching the sun set over West Lake. Not great in the rain, so fingers crossed for good weather.

If you like to indulge in a massage or three, Hanoi has a fair few spas. As usual, the Sofitel Metropole is the most indulgent, but others, including Zen Spa and Santal Spa on Xuan Dieu Street and Vincharm at Vincom Towers offer quality treatments as well.

Finally and back to food check out one of the two top steak restaurants in Hanoi: Jacksons and El Gaucho Argentinian Steakhouse. At the latter, world-class steaks run from a reasonable 450,000 VND up to 3 million VND if you can eat a kilo of fillet. Let us know if you do. If steak's not your thing, both offer other options, or try one of the other top end restaurants: Halia, Pots n Pans, La Verticale and La Badiane, to name but a few.

Which is the best street food tour in Hanoi?

After four tours, approximately 13 kilometres of walking, three portions of banh cuon, a kilo of extra weight and enough sugar to dissolve a few dozen teeth, my food tour adventure in Hanoi is over. It's reinvigorated my love of street food and inspired me to try a few new places, but which was the best?

When money's no object

Following the old-adage of "you get what you pay for", if budget was not a consideration then without question I would go on the priciest tour, Hanoi Street Food Tours. In fact, when our next big pay cheque comes in I'm going to encourage my boyfriend to go on it as I enjoyed it so much. It wasn't just the food, much of which was new to me, but also Mark's (or Tu's) agreeable company and wealth of knowledge.

But there's no denying it's expensive: despite inflation, US$75 gets you a lot in Hanoi, and perhaps dinner at one of the city's top restaurants holds more appeal. Me, though, I'd opt for their street food tour.

Avoiding the crowds

If you want a more budget-friendly tour then you'll need to join a group. Three of the tours I tried were group ones, with participants ranging in number from three to five guests, although all would take up to eight. Three is a good number, five is pushing it, and eight would be too many.

Bigger groups might be just about fine when you're sitting at a table, eating, but in reality a lot of time is spent walking around hectic Old Quarter and it can be difficult to pick up on information offered by the guide if there are too many people standing around.

And, of course, street food stalls aren't generally set up for large groups, unless you're eating hotpot or at a bia hoi joint. Unfortunately you don't get to influence the number of guests and might end up in a larger group; so if you don't like crowds, stump up and opt for a private tour.

As well as Hanoi Street Food Tour, which only provides private tours, Well Eaten Path (with Daniel Hoyer) offers a private tour option and Vietnam Awesome Travel's Food on Foot tour can be taken as a private tour for US$38, so is worth considering as a cheaper alternative.

Food versus tour of Old Quarter

One of the reasons that the Hanoi Cooking Centre tour was so good is that the guide –- a KOTO-trained chef was evidently passionate and knowledgeable about food and really enhanced the experience: this was all about the food, with no distractions. The same was true of the Hanoi Street Food Tour.

The Food on Foot tour managed to achieve a reasonable balance between being an introduction to street food, the Old Quarter and the history of Vietnam: our guide didn't have a particular passion for food, but knew her stuff and the ad hoc stops to try food on sale along the street was a nice touch. The Urban Adventures tour was similar in concept, in that it merged a walking tour with eating, but somehow fell too far on the side of walking tour of Old Quarter to really feel like a street food adventure. Of these two, which are similarly priced, the

Food on Foot tour comes more highly recommended from us (more food stops for a start).

Hidden spots or tourist traps

It's inevitable that tours will sometimes end up at well-documented venues. Inevitable in part because these are often well-known spots for a reason: the food's good. Also, some tour operators are keen to stick to places that have been vetted and offer a certain level of hygiene.

For some, this is a perfect introduction street food with security –- but what about if you've already dipped your toe in the world of *pho* and *bun cha* and are looking for a tour that can show you the real off-the-beaten track spots and introduce you to new dishes? This is a very subjective area, as off-the-beaten track for some might be everyday and boring for others. To generalise, however, the two more expensive tours went to less touristy places. Of course, if you have specific requests -food you want to try or to avoid -you'll need to book onto a private tour and discuss your requirements in advance.

Although I didn't test it out again, the short tours from Hidden Hanoi - which I reviewed in August 2011 –- take place outside of Old Quarter, although try quite standard dishes such as pho and *bun cha*.

Where the food comes from

A wet market, or street market, should be a must-see on any visit to Vietnam, certainly for a foodie, and visiting with a knowledgeable guide is recommended. So it makes sense to include it with a street food tour.

The market tour with Hanoi Cooking Centre was excellent: it was a real tour, rather than a quick walk through, as Y took time to show us different produce and prompt us to try tasters. A market visit, or two, are also included with Hanoi Street Food Tours' itinerary.

Urban Adventures' Hanoi Street Food by Night tour includes a walk around the outskirts of Dong Xuan market and the nearby street market. It's lively and interesting to observe, but no commentary was provided on the tour I took, except when prompted. The Foot on Foot tour didn't include a market visit.

In summary

Because the tours are all different, in terms of price and time of day, and you'll all be turned on by different things, it's difficult to make a one-size-fits-all recommendation. Quality decreases as price decreases, but that's not to say that you should avoid the cheaper options.

The Food on Foot tour was a close comparison to Hanoi Cooking Centre's offer, at half the price, but it did lack the market visit and the benefit of having a chef as a guide. With no doubt though, we highly recommend doing some kind of street food tour while you're in Hanoi: read our posts, see what sounds good and book on!

Shopping

Shopping in Hanoi

Hanoi offers superb shopping, from interesting Vietnamese tourist trinkets (or tat, depending on your perspective) through to stunning, world-class art, and almost everything in between: think historic propaganda posters, water puppets, traditional musical instruments, hand-crafted quilts, Bat Trang's famous ceramics, coffee filters as well as coffee ... the list is long. Buy that extra baggage allowance!

Shopping locations in Hanoi vary widely too, from traditional markets and jam-packed holes in the wall, through to glass-fronted boutiques and air-conditioned malls. Consider the following merely an introduction to get you hunting. Places come and go, though some have been around for a few generations.

For your basic tourist souvenirs, such as T-shirts, flags, silk scarves, lanterns, fridge magnets and so on, Old Quarter is packed to the gills with little shops. Prices may be marked or not; if they aren't, you may haggle, remembering to keep it friendly and fun for the best results. In general, offer half the asking price; then expect to meet the vendor around half way between the two. One unusual item to keep an eye out for that we like are personalised stamps, an ideal gift for that someone who seemingly has everything.

Old Quarter's Hang Gai, or Silk Street, is the place to head for good-quality silk and tailors. In particular along this stretch, you'll find Tan My Design, one of the most beautiful standalone shops in Hanoi, its plate-glass frontage giving a glimpse of the treasures within its two storeys. Here you'll find silk as well as a range of higher-end souvenirs. Opened in 2009, it's a genuine emporium, boasting an excellent selection of jewellery, clothes, lacquerware and tableware. Many of the items here have been created by some of Vietnam's best designers. There's an in-house cafe if you need a break (though to be honest our pick would be somewhere else Old Quarter with more atmosphere).

Hanoi's 36 streets

The 36 streets of Hanoi's Old Quarter spread over a small area, but just try spending time here without getting lost! Here's a rundown of some of the main streets and what you can find there.

But first, some background. Back in the day around the 13th century, give or take these streets became hectic with (possibly) 36 humming artisan guilds, either being established to provide goods to the emperor, or to trade with merchants, depending on who you read. Each guild was built surrounding its own temple dedicated to its patron spirit. The Old Quarter back then was gated and protected behind ramparts; only the eastern gate remains standing today.

Some streets still specialise in selling certain objects, but only a few remain properly faithful to their original craft. Some of the original streets and their merchandise include Cho Gau for rice, Hang But for brushes, Hang Huong for incense and Hang Than for charcoal.

The etymology of the 36 behind the 36 streets is unclear. Some believe there may have in fact been 36 guilds originally, but it's also possible the 36 derives from four times nine, where four refers to north, south, east and west, and nine represents plenty

These days aside from some 70 or so streets in the Old Quarter, there are plenty more little alleys to wander around, too. While you wander, keep an eye out (and up) for tube houses, originally built with very narrow fronts and long rooms stretching back from the street in order for the owners to avoid paying property taxes based on street frontage. Houses were also restricted to being two-storeys high in deference to the palace and any passing royalty. A good example is 87

Buying a secondhand motorbike

If you are planning a long roadtrip, or one that doesn't start and end in Hanoi, it's likely to be more economical to buy a motorbike rather than rent. Here's a rundown of where to buy a secondhand bike in Hanoi. Do remember that if you don't have a local license, your travel insurance may be invalid do check ahead of your trip. Here's a rundown of where to buy a secondhand bike in Hanoi.

A good place to start in Old Quarter is Ngo Huyen, the lane that runs between Ly Quoc Su and Phu Doan streets. Home to a number of backpacker-style hostels and guesthouses it's a popular place for new arrivals at the end of their adventure to park their trusted steeds and stick up a FOR SALE sign.

Also check hostel noticeboards and do ask around enjoying a few beers with other travellers will likely bring you into contact with someone selling a bike.

Some vendors, including expats, will also post an advert on TNH (Hanoi's primary expat website) so keep an eye on the classifieds there.

It's useful to have a phone with a local SIM card to facilitate contact, as most people will only leave a phone number and it's quicker than sending an email.

A few motorbike rental places also sell bikes from time to time and may be a safer bet than buying off the street. Rentabike regularly sells on old rentals, which are listed on its website and come with a one-month warranty. They're mostly Waves and Nuovos. VIP Bikes is primarily a rental and repair place but very occasionally refurbs classic bikes or has old rentals for sale.

Off Road Vietnam is a tour and rental place which apparently sells on old rentals, but none were available when we last got in touch. Also check out the eastern end of Luong Ngoc Quyen near the Irish Wolfhound where a few bike tour places are located.

If you're after something custom built or refurbished, contact Kub Cafe: it might take some time to get exactly what you want but if you're not in a rush the end result will be worth it.

The most common bikes found for sale are Minsks and Honda Wins (manuals), Honda Waves (semi-automatic) and Yamaha Nuovos (automatic). They're all quite different in terms of driving style and comfort, so before searching for a bike think about what type of bike will best suit your needs. Make sure you get a registration card when you buy the bike too it won't be in your name but you will need it if stopped by police.

It's possible to buy a new Honda Wave for under US$1,000 but registration can take some time and requires a lot of paperwork plus the bike will devalue notably as soon as you drive away from the showroom, so secondhand is the more practical option.

Day trips
Perfume Pagoda

The sprawling Perfume Pagoda, or Chua Huong, is a series of revered shrines and temples tucked into the pretty Huong Tich mountains, a few hours' drive out of Hanoi.

The sacred pagoda is popular with Vietnamese devotees year round, but particularly from the middle of the second to the end of the third lunar months following Tet, and on even days of the lunar calendar. Embrace the madness and see how a Vietnamese tourism destination operates: think lots of noise, souvenirs galore and plenty of snacks and food. This is arguably the mother of all domestic tourism spots in Vietnam, and should be experienced for that reason alone, whether you learn anything about Buddhism along the way or not.

The first temple on the site here is thought to have been built in the 1400s, though legend has it that the area was found by a meditating monk more than 2,000 years ago. A stele uncovered at the current temple dates the building of a terrace and stone steps to the mid-17th century; sections of the grounds were damaged by both the French and the American wars.

The Perfume Pagoda trip is one of the main day trips hawked by tour agencies in Hanoi. Priced from $25 up to around $39 for VIP service, they kick off with a hotel pick up around 08:00 to 08:30 and get back after dark, around 19:00 or 19:30, depending on traffic.

You'll drive a few hours, stopping for a bathroom break en route at a souvenir shop where you can also buy your own drinks and snacks, then stop at a boat pier where rowers pilot blue light steel boats taking either six Westerners or 25-plus Vietnamese tourist for the 45-minute river trip to the base of the pagoda. Many tourists often take the paddles and row for a stretch, mostly for the photo op. It's all very peaceful and pleasant, until you meet a boat that has purchased blow horns to toot up and down

Booking a Ha Long Bay cruise

With more than 400 boats to choose from, selecting a Ha Long Bay tour is tricky enough to start with. Throw in the third party travel agents and hotel tour desks who can quote whatever they want for a cruise and it's a minefield. Here are some tips to get the best for your buck.

First decide how much you want to spend. Although you can pick up a Ha Long Bay cruise for almost any budget, boats can be broadly grouped into budget (under US$60), three-star ($60-$110), four-star ($110-160) and five-star plus ($160+), with prices based on a two-day, one-night cruise with an overnight stay on the boat.

Three-day tours jump the price up by around 40 percent, so balance your budget with how long you want to spend in the Bay. Agents will probably try to talk you up to a higher level particularly if you go in looking for something cheap but don't believe everything they tell you and don't believe the photos in the brochure, especially for the cheaper options.

It was harder than we expected to get a cheap tour. Some agents were happy to provide details of the budget tours when requested, but others started with a pricier option and only offered the cheaper version when pushed. Or they simply didn't have cheap boats on their books we only found three operators under US$50. Our trusted travel agent has a budget boat she can put people on if that's all they are interested in, but she always makes its shortcomings in comfort, service and safety clear.

The flashpacker tours weren't vying for attention either. Du Gong Sails was the dominant one offered in the US$60-100 price range, with others including Papaya, Elizabeth Sails and the Halong Party Cruise. Once you get above US$100 the options open up.

You have a few options for booking a tour. Book online in advance direct with the operator; book online with Agoda; book with your hotel in advance or on arrival in Hanoi; book with a local travel agent on arrival; or book with a travel agent in your home country especially suitable if you're booking a package tour.

Which way to book is best? It's hard to say, though it depends what you're after. If you're looking for a cheap deal then you're probably best off visiting some agents when you get to Hanoi. The cheapest deals we found on line were US$80+, but you can pick up overnight tours for as little as US$45 from an agent in Old Quarter. White Sails, for example, is US$75 online at the time of writing, but around US$50 from an agent.

If price isn't an issue and you want a decent boat, then doing online research from home and booking online direct with an operator, via a local agent or with a site like Agoda, is an easier option. Make sure you compare prices across the booking options. It's not always cheapest to book direct with the operator as agents get good deals.

Even if you want to keep your schedule loose and prefer to book with an agent when you arrive, it's worth doing some research in advance so you have a shortlist and an idea of prices. Then, on arrival, shop around a bit.

We visited a heap of agents in Old Quarter and prices for the same boat differed by up to US$30 for an overnight cruise. For example, Sinh Cafe Tourist at 52-53b Luong Ngoc Quyen and Friendly Travel on Ma May charged US$85 for Du Gong Sails a decent flashpacker option whereas we got it for $75. Likewise, Vietnam Impressive wanted US$115 for the four-star Galaxy but a couple of doors down they were charging US$140. Note that prices can change even on a daily basis depending on how busy the boat is.

In summary, do your research and shop around. Don't take everything at face value. And read our reviews (links are earlier in this piece)!

Two or three days in Ha Long Bay?

When planning your trip to Vietnam, it can be a challenge to fit everything in, and one of the questions you may well ask yourself is how long to spend in Ha Long Bay. While this is a personal choice, here's our view.

The options for organised tours from Hanoi rather than travelling independently are one, two or three days. On a two-day trip you can either stay on the boat or on Cat Ba Island, while the three-day trips generally offer the choice of either staying on the boat for two nights or one night on the boat and one on Cat Ba Island.

Let's start by saying that we wouldn't recommend a day trip. It's a lot of driving approximately four hours each way in a minibus for very little time in the Bay. So yes, you can take some pictures and say you've been there, but you're likely to end the day exhausted and not as rewarded as you may have hoped. However, we're pragmatists if you really only have one day and don't mind the potentially cramped minibus scenario, then go for it. But try to avoid the budget tours so you at least get a decent lunch.

We reckon a two-day, one-night trip is long enough to enjoy the view, partake in a few activities and absorb the atmosphere. But stay on the boat, not on Cat Ba. Cat Ba is a great place to explore and spend a few days but we'd rate a night on the boat as a more fulfilling experience. Bear in mind, however, that you may not get too much time to chill out on deck on a two-day tour as the boat operators seem obsessed with filling every moment with an activity. So if that's important to you, be careful to check out the itinerary.

When it comes to the three-day option, some think it's too long, while others enjoy the more relaxed pace and variety of activities on offer. Another benefit is that you get to cruise deeper into the Bay. Ask your travel agent to show you the route and make sure the boat goes as far as Bai Tu Long Bay or Lan Ha Bay. If you opt for one night on the boat and one night on Cat Ba, your tour will likely include a walk in the national park, which will appeal to some, and may include a bike ride or village tour. Some also offer the option to visit Monkey Island.

You may also have some time to explore Cat Ba Island on your own if you skip Monkey Island for example but again, check the itinerary first if this is important to you.

Some operators now offer a stay on a private island for the second night. This may appeal more to you if you want to relax in a hammock or on the beach, or participate in water sports. Operators providing this option include Hanoi Backpackers' Hostel and Classy Travel.

Overall, if time and budget are not an issue, we'd recommend two nights, with one spent on Cat Ba Island or a private island two nights on the boat could be a bit dull. Why two nights? Firstly, it gets you deeper into the Bay, where it's more beautiful and less crowded though don't expect solitude and secondly, you'll have the chance to do more activities and explore a bit of Cat Ba Island (as well as eat the amazing seafood); thirdly, it is more relaxing; and finally, it gives you a break from the bus. But if it's all about the Bay and you have little interest in additional activities, one night should do you just fine.

A final note, if the weather's wet, we'd change our suggestion to two days, but as it's so hard to predict the weather in Ha Long you'll just have to take your chances we're afraid.

Hanoi to Mai Chau by motorbike

At 139 kilometres from Hanoi, Mai Chau is a popular two- or three-day trip from Hanoi. Having squeezed onto over-crowded, under air-conditioned buses on previous trips, on our latest soujourn we decided to jump on motorbikes and cruise there at our own pace, wind in our hair, sun on our backs and all that. Was it worth it? Yes. Is it for everyone? No. Here's why.

The first thing you should bear in mind if setting out on a motorbike trip anywhere outside of Hanoi is that you have to drive through a lot of busy and dirty urban sprawl before you get to the peaceful, scenic roads. Fortunately Mai Chau is southwest of the city, so one of the main roads out it's not the shortest but it's our preferred option is the newly refurbished and relatively quiet Thang Long highway. However, you'll still have to navigate some rather hairy roads either side of the highway before you reach the more rural areas. Wear a face mask and drive carefully.

We opted to drive via Hoa Binh and return via back roads. We'd recommend the latter you can cut through from the QL6 west of Xuan Mai to the QL6 south of Hoa Binh. Both routes are interesting and scenic but the back roads have slightly less traffic and are more peaceful.

It's unfortunate that the route to Mai Chau is popular with trucks and buses, because without them the drive would be much more pleasant. Nonetheless, the moments that made the drive worthwhile for us included the drive on the back roads and the drive up into the mountains, which is around the last hour of the drive. Note that even on a hot day it can get a bit chilly at the top of the pass so you may need something warmer than a vest top and if the clouds are low you may have to slow down for a while.

The views from the mountain road when not cloudy are quite spectacular in places; keep an eye out for the viewpoint as you start heading down towards Mai Chau. Also look out for a rest stop at the highest point, where women sell sticky rice in bamboo and corn-on-the-cob good views and food to boot.

In reality, if you're not pushing it and are stopping for food and drink breaks en route, you need to allow five hours each way. That's quite a lot of driving and we'd highly recommend you stay at least two nights in Mai Chau to make the most of the journey and to give your bum time to recover.

On the subject of food and drink breaks: as long as you're happy with noodles or rice plus, eaten in non-salubrious surroundings, you'll find somewhere to stop along the way. We stopped in Hoa Binh for a noodle soup lunch and took a couple of other breaks for coffee and cold drinks.

We'd recommend joining a tour if you're on your own, not just for the company but also for safety. While getting your bike fixed at the roadside may be feasible, getting yourself fixed up if you're unfortunate enough to come off the bike is not, so having companions is a good idea. Also, don't forget that your insurance will likely be invalid if you don't have a Vietnamese driving license.

In summary, Hanoi to Mai Chau by motorbike is far from an easy drive and is very tiring, but it's a doable drive in terms of distance and road quality; if the weather's good and you're confident and comfortable on a bike, it beats the crowded buses. With a group and with enough stops for rest and fuel food and drink, not petrol it's an adventurous and fun excursion from Hanoi.

For the fit with some time on their hands, do as our friend did and go by bicycle then you really will need two nights in Mai Chau for your bum to recover!

Bat Trang ceramic village

Home to the pottery families of Hanoi, Bat Trang village is also referred to as the ceramic village and makes for an easy half-day excursion from the city. It's one of numerous old villages on the outskirts of the capital that have specialised in a range of cottage industries for centuries.

Bat Trang has been producing earthenware since the 15th century, and is best known for its blue-and-white designs, though these days the 2,000 or so families based here produce a range of ceramic styles, as well as more functional bricks and tiles for export. While it used to be worth the trek here to pick up well-priced souvenirs, we reckon these days the range and cost is comparable back in Hanoi, and you can easily skip a visit without too much regret.

Shops selling merchandise ranging from the traditional blue and white plates and bowls to more modern designs start as soon as you enter the village off the main road. Follow this road along for a kilometre or so until you reach the main market ("cho"). A traditional coal-fired kiln is in operation just by the market, but signs strictly forbid entering and photography; most of the several thousand kilns here these days are gas-fired, but we still saw dried coal-pats being dislodged from walls to use as fuel.

The shops in the village seem more suited to tour groups one shop had everything priced in yen though they certainly sell retail to anyone. One shop attendant warned us that a lot of the ceramics are now imported from China, and said to only buy products marked with "Bat Trang" underneath. Whether this was a sales tactic or the truth, it did seem like the items so marked were of a higher quality.

An overnight trip to Tam Dao

While not a must-visit destination, if you're not in a rush and are keen to explore less touristy spots in Vietnam, Tam Dao hill station is worth an overnight from Hanoi, especially to escape the capital's summer heat. Here's some advice on how to spend your time there.

Leave Hanoi after breakfast by bus, bike or car to get to Tam Dao in time for lunch. Places to eat and drink line the streets, so if you're a fan of Vietnamese food you'll be spoiled for choice. If you're not a fan, simply grilled yet tasty meat is easy to find and the town is famous for its *su su* a leafy green vegetable served boiled (*luoc*) or fried (*xao*) with garlic. Other specialties include deer, squirrel, porcupine and boar.

Check into your hotel and change into walking shoes it's all about walking in Tam Dao. Head along the main road up the hill until you reach a gate, where you'll need to pay the guard 25,000 VND admission to continue; it's a bit of a walk to get there, or on a motorbike it takes around 10 minutes. Once past the gate, you'll begin about a two-hour walk through bamboo forest with the occasional 180-degree view of the forest below. The path can get muddy, but is well-signposted and you're unlikely to come across anyone else, making it a peaceful and interesting walk.

For a shorter walk, visit the waterfall, near the Mela Hotel, or, in summer, spend the afternoon at the public swimming pool in the centre of town.

Tam Dao is not a place to go looking for a party unless you're a fan of Vietnamese karaoke, which seems to be very popular but street food stalls selling delights including kebabs, baked eggs, chicken feet and corn run alongside the river, near the market, and are a good place to start, and maybe end, the night.

As the food on offer at the stalls is unlikely to satiate a hearty appetite, head to one of the many restaurants for some more meat and su su and, if you're brave enough, some rice wine. Check out the rice wine variants at Kim Lien restaurant, near Gia Le Hotel the grilled pork is highly recommended but the snake rice wine is not.

Next day, after breakfast at your hotel or a local restaurant, wander down to the market square to see vendors selling both to locals meat and eggs and tourists rugs, scarves and the like. Enjoy a Vietnamese coffee at one of the cafes at the northern end of the public pool; expect to pay 10,000 VND for a strong cafe sua (coffee with milk).

Explore the rest of the town. Despite recent development, many interesting buildings remain. They may be rundown and shabby, but that somehow adds to their appeal.

Consider a stop at Tay Thien Pagoda, sometimes called the birth place of Vietnamese Buddhism, and home to some wonderful mountain pagodas, on the way back to Hanoi if you have time.

As for when to go, at 920 metres above sea level, the weather in Tam Dao is far cooler than in Hanoi, so it's a pleasant respite from the heat in the summer but in the winter you'll need to wrap up, particularly in the evenings. On the positive side, despite the cold, the weather in winter is lovely, with blue skies and low humidity.

At 80 kilometres northwest of Hanoi, you can reach Tam Dao by bus, motorbike, taxi or private car; here's a little about how to do each.

Usually the cheapest option for getting to Tam Dao is to go by public bus, from Gia Lam bus station, but they only run as far as Vinh Yen, from where you'll need to take a taxi or motorbike taxi the last 24-kilometre stretch.

If you want total flexibility, at relatively low cost, then go by motorbike (but remember you need a licenseto be legal and insured). Unfortunately, as is always the way when getting out of Hanoi, you have to battle through the pollution and crazy traffic before you reach any notable scenery or signs of serenity, but once you get off the highway it's an enjoyable enough ride. Expect to be on the road for around three hours.

First head out of town on the dyke road this is the main road that runs to the east of Old Quarter and keeps on going… Eventually you will reach the Thanh Long Bridge, which traverses the Red River. The route to get onto the bridge is a bit convoluted but follow motorbike (xe may) signs and you'll be fine.

From the other side of the bridge, the most direct, but less pretty, route takes you almost all the way to Noi Bai International Airport on the main highway, then turns left onto another large road towards Vinh Yen. Turn right at the big roundabout as you enter Vinh Yen then continue onto the next large roundabout where you turn right again onto a peaceful yet wide road called Duong Tam Dao. From there you can see Tam Dao hill station and it's an easy, signposted route.

For a more scenic ride, and if you're feeling brave or have GPS, take the first turning that's signposted Phuc Yen, shortly after Thang Long Bridge. From there, explore the back roads to make your way to Tam Dao. The last 10 kilometres or so of the journey is particularly scenic, although steep. If you're heading up with a passenger, make sure your bike's got a decent engine or take good walking shoes. And expect it to take a while as you'll want to stop for photos.

If motorbikes aren't your thing, how about cycling? A good degree of fitness is essential, particularly for the last climb, but you'll certainly deserve the cold beer at the end.

Given the distance from Hanoi, it's also feasible to take a taxi without breaking the bank. A small Mai Linh will cost around 800,000 VND (US$40) each way it's not bad if there are a few of you, although a bigger taxi will hike the price up to over 1 million VND. If you've been practising your Vietnamese you might even be able to negotiate a stop off en route for a coffee or lunch.

If you want more flexibility and have a bigger budget, then consider hiring a car. A day trip will run to around US$60 and overnight US$80. Or organise a tour through an agent. Group tours aren't common so you'll need to arrange a private tour, but it's a hassle-free alternative. Most travel agents and hotels will be able to help, although True Colour Tour comes recommended and I've successfully organised car hire with Golden Package Tour (hawkhuong1982gpt@gmail.com).

Cu Da, or Vermicelli Village

After my enjoyable visit to Bamboo Village (Bang So) I was really looking forward to the trip to Vermicelli Village (Cu Da); I love food and am always keen to learn more about it.

I was not disappointed, as not only was it fascinating to see and hear about the production of vermicelli but I found Cu Da to be an interesting and friendly spot.

Vermicelli noodles are called *mien* in Vietnamese and come in white and yellow versions. They are used mainly in noodle soup and in fried spring rolls.

Both white and yellow versions are made with arrowroot. The arrowroot is ground and mixed with water to make a paste which is spread onto large bamboo trays and dried. It is then cut into thin strips the vermicelli and dried again before being packaged. Although machines are now used for the spreading and cutting, it's still a very labour-intensive process. Half of the village's income comes from vermicelli production.

Cu Da is in what was originally Ha Tay province but is now part of ever-expanding Hanoi. It's about 20km south of the centre of Hanoi on the banks of the river Nhu. The area has changed notably in even the past 10 years, with urbanisation making it more of a suburb than a village; and sadly the river is no longer the clean, beautiful trading route it once was but is dead and rather smelly.

That said, Cu Da still has a lot to recommend to the visitor. Of course, there's the vermicelli, but it's also home to an interesting mix of architecture: traditional housing, tube houses, French influences and modern homes. In addition its main temple, Chua Cu Da, is attractive and well-kept and other cultural and interesting buildings are dotted here and there, such as the communal village house, family temples, the public well and hamlet gates. The people also seemed particularly friendly, perhaps typical of out-of-centre locations.

The easiest and best way to visit is on a tour. It's hassle-free and really worth having a good guide who can not only show you around but talk to you more widely about the culture of Vietnam and the villages. I travelled with Exotissimo on a large group tour and my guide was Dan. They don't run very often but it's worth getting in touch as they will organise private tours as well.

If you prefer to do it alone, it's feasible to get there by bus, taxi or motorbike from Hanoi. To do so, head out of town on Ton Duc Thang (alongside the Temple of Literature) and follow this for a few kilometres it changes name twice until you get to the flyover. Go over the flyover and keep going straight for quite some time. Keep an eye out for Song Nhue Hotel on the right it's a big yellow building and turn left onto Duong Phung Hung. Continue along this road for a good few kilometres, this time looking out for the river and a dam on the left hand side. Just after the dam there's a Petrolimex petrol station (there's also one before the dam, but ignore that one). Take the right turn almost opposite the Petrolimex onto Ta Thanh Oai. The road becomes much narrower now. Continue to follow it until you get to the railway bridge, on the right. Jump out here if you're in a taxi.

If you're going by bus, get the No. 2 from Hoan Kiem to Ha Dong bus station on Nguyen Trai after the flyover where you can pick up the No. 37. That takes you along Duong Phung Hung so you'll need to watch out for the dam and Petrolimex, and jump off on the main road then find a xe om or taxi to take you the rest of the way or walk the three or so kilometres along Ta Thanh Oai to the railway bridge.

Once there, cross the railway bridge then turn right across the tracks, with the river on your left, and take the first right to see a factory spreading paste onto bamboo trays. Backtrack and walk along the road parallel to the river. Take the next right and if you continue to follow this road you'll come across a similar factory but this time making white vermicelli. Note the small cutting machines on the floor. If you continue on this road you will see an old house down an alley on the left on my visit they were very welcoming and then a large public well which villagers traditionally took drinking water from.

At the T-junction turn right back onto the river road and you'll pass the communal village house, the gateway to Xom Chua hamlet, a family temple and finally, the main village temple. If you miss the right turn mentioned above, take the right just before the village house and do that loop in reverse.

Motorbike trips

There has been a motorbike-supply eruption in Hanoi in recent years, with numerous operators offering not only bike rental and sales but also organised tours. Here's the lowdown.

While it's of course possible to replicate the trips they offer under your own steam, a guided tour provides companionship, security and most likely a better route than you'll find on your own. And of course, there'll be no arguments over which way up the map goes. With tours including accommodation and food, they can also take the stress out of planning and ensure you get a good feed.

You can choose between private and group tours. A private tour means you just go with the people you book with, rather than joining a group of strangers. They tend to be more expensive, but can be tailored to your needs. Single travellers or those on a budget may prefer to join a group tour. Groups are kept to a comfortable size, so you won't be trailing down Highway 1 in convoy, but still provide an opportunity to meet others, and the cost is usually lower.

Popular overnight and two-night trips from Hanoi include Mai Chau, Ninh Binh, Tam Dao and Cuc Phuong National Park. Thac Ba Lake is another, less visited, nearby option. If you want to venture further afield, north Vietnam offers numerous routes through amazing scenery, or buy a bike and do the classic north-to-south journey.

Rentabike remain a good bet for bike rentals and now also operate private guided tours for groups of two or more and will help you plan an itinerary if you want to go it alone. Prices range from US$80 to $140 per day, all inclusive.

Dao Duy Tu and Luong Ngoc Quyen Streets in Old Quarter are now lined with motorbike shops, a popular spot being Vietnam Motorbikes. Originally focused on refurbishing and selling bikes, they now also offer guided tours. Their two-day tours cost US$80 per person, including bike hire, accommodation, food and a guide, and they guarantee no more than six bikes on each tour. Choose from automatic, semi-automatic or "beefed up" manuals.

Famous Cuong's Motorbike Adventures now operates out of a smart shop on Gia Ngu Street, also in Old Quarter, and has a diverse fleet of motorbikes on which to enjoy your tour. Bikes include Minsks, Urals and more modern Honda CRFs. Cuong's offers a range of scheduled departures on trips lasting from three to 11 days and can also arrange trips as far as Ho Chi Minh City or into Laos.

Finally although this list is by no means exhaustive the tours on offer by Zoom Zoom Let's Go to the Countryside include motorbike trips to northern destinations including Mai Chau and Ha Giang.

Cuong's Motorbike Adventures 46 Gia Ngu St, T: (0918) 763 515 cuongs-motorbike-adventure.com

Rentabike 6b Tam Thuong St and 27 / 52 To Ngoc Van St. T: (0913) 026 878;(0904) 392 423 www.rentabikehanoi.com

Vietnam Motorbikes 40 Dao Duy Tu St, T: (01662) 913 512. vietnam-motorbikes@gmail.com

Dau pagoda and Horn village

Dau pagoda, considered Vietnam's oldest, is located 24 kilometres south of the centre of Hanoi, in Bac Ninh province, and takes about one hour to reach by road.

In the third century, the area in which it is located was the capital of Giai Chi, at the time Vietnam's political, economic and cultural centre. Khau Da La, an Indian monk, visited the area to do missionary work and founded the first Buddhism centre in Vietnam, called Luy Lau, and many pagodas were built, including Dau. Although the Dau pagoda is dedicated to Buddhism, the Goddess of Clouds and the Goddess of Rains are worshipped here too.

Although much has been destroyed and re-built or renovated over the years, the pagoda retains numerousstriking architectural details and houses a wide range of Buddha statues and other antiques.

Besides its age, another of its claims to fame are its mummies of two monks, Vu Khac Minh and Vu Khac Truong, which date from the 17th century and were re-discovered in 1983. One body is coated in layers of gold and paint and the other in silver and paint.

The new area at the back of the pagoda is an oasis of calm, with benches set in the shade of numerous trees, ponds and streams, temples and a statue of Quan In, the protector against accidents. Also look for the stone lotus flowers which form steps across the pond: the seven flowers represent the first seven steps a baby Buddha takes.

Despite its importance, the pagoda is usually quiet, only coming to life on special days, such as the Dau pagoda festival, which falls annually around May. There's little else around, although the ubiquitous drinks stall sits near the entrance if you need to quench your thirst.

The pagoda can easily be viewed in an hour, so it makes for a half-day trip from Hanoi; however, all but the hardened pagoda fan will perhaps feel it's a bit too much effort and expense to just visit one sight. So consider a stop in Horn village (Thuy Ung), a few kilometres away. There's not much to see there now in terms of horn craft but it's a pleasant enough village.

Firstly, find the square pond in the centre of the village. Walk around it anti-clockwise and on the second corner after the small pagoda is a house where they still flatten the horns. There are sacks of buffalo horns waiting to be soaked in oil and flattened ready to be made into combs and other articles. Retrace your steps and continue straight before passing the pagoda again to reach Ung Xa Tu Pagoda and the Community House.

On the road out of the village are a few shops manufacturing and selling fake animal heads made from plastic and coated with fur, with real horns not to our taste but it's apparently a lucrative market.

As with most of the outlying pagodas and villages, it's advisable to plan a trip via a travel agent, not just for ease of transport but for the added value an informative guide can offer. A number of agents in Hanoi can organise private tours to the pagoda and other sights in the area.

If you want to make your own way take Giai Phong out of town, turn right in Thuong Tin onto TL71 then left and follow the road with the river on your right. You can take a bus along the main road but will have to take a taxi or xe om the last few kilometres.

Other sights in Bach Ninh include Viem Xa village, Do Temple in Dinh Bang village, and Phu Lang Pottery village.

Overall, Dau Pagoda is certainly worthy of a visit if you have a particular interest in pagodas or are passing that way, although its location and the cost of a guided tour is likely to be off-putting for most.

Bang So (Bamboo village)

In the past, villagers in Vietnam tended to specialise in making particular items to meet their needs, sharing their skills with neighbours and relatives. This led to individual villages becoming known for a particular handicraft. As people moved to the cities they gravitated towards others with the same trade and hence we have areas such as Hanoi's Old Quarter, where different streets specialised in certain items.

Although, as with the Old Quarter's 36 streets, many villages no longer practice, or at least rely on, their original trade, there are still plenty of opportunities to visit handicraft villages around Hanoi to watch artisans at work and buy their wares.

Bat Trang ceramic village and Van Phuc silk village are probably the best known, but there's also Ninh Hiep fabric village, Ha Thai lacquer village, Chuong conical hat village and many more. The one I most recently visited was Bang So bamboo village.

Bang So is about 20km from the centre of Hanoi, south along the 'dyke' road the main road that runs along the east of Old Quarter. Although the road starts smooth it gets bumpier as it heads out of the centre and passes through suburban towns and past paddy fields. So although the easiest way to get there is by motorbike wear a facemask, it's dusty I'd question the suitability of the road for novice drivers.

If you're not going by motorbike then you can either take a taxi, which will cost 200,000 VND+ each way depending upon the size, or you can go on an organised tour: many operators offer a village tour package which covers Bat Trang (ceramic village) and Bang So, saving you the trouble of finding the workshops and negotiating the potholes though of course for many that may be part of the fun.

Before I go on I'm going to dispel any romantic images you may have of a handicraft village: unfortunately you will not find a pretty collection of traditional houses with villagers sitting around practising their trade and waiting to sell the pot / basket / scarf they have just made to you for a wholesale bargain price. Villages have grown, some have even been absorbed into the growing urban sprawl of Hanoi, and, in the case of the bamboo village at least, artisans are now spread out throughout the village and take a bit of finding.

That said, I don't want to put you off exploring: I spent a good morning there. The places we visited were all near the main road, either facing the road (although down the embankment) or on one of the side roads, but without street names I'm afraid I'm unable to give you precise locations.

First we visited a woman who was making twee baskets in her living room, and down the alley behind her house was a larger, open-air operation making similar items.

Next was onto a small workshop where they made some attractive and unusual lampshades, and then opposite to another basket-making home set-up. We then walked along the path next to the main road and went into a warehouse-style building: there was nothing being made when we visited but there were heaps of large sacks filled with goodies. I picked up some bamboo bowls and colourful storage boxes great Christmas presents.

Our last stop was at a place where they make a wide range of goods, mostly for export. This included some very attractive laundry baskets and, perhaps more exciting, handbags. Prices are quite high and there's no room for negotiation they don't seem to really care about drop in trade, but are all about the export but it was worth a stop to oooh over the nicely-made items.

Exploring Bac Kan province

You don't always have to stick to the tourist trail in Vietnam; simply striking out somewhere for the hell of it can be richly rewarding. Bac Kan province is little visited by tourists, although its main point of interest, Ba Be Lake, attracts those looking for natural beauty outside of Ha Long Bay.

We took a wander through the area recently and savoured the flavour of rural Vietnamese life. Bac Kan is an ethnic and mountainous province one of the poorest in Vietnam. In fact in 2009 it had the highest poverty rate in the country, with an average monthly per capita income of 669,000 VND.

Most of its income is from agriculture, but this is primarily small scale, household farming, rather than mass commercial production; so although the majority of households grow, breed or collect something, most of this is used for living, rather the for sale.

Corn is widespread, and can be seen hanging everywhere to dry. The corn isn't eaten but is dried, split into kernels and then either made into paste by the householders to feed their own animals, or sold on. It sells for around 5,000 VND per kilogram.

Ginger is a good crop for the province as it's easy to grow and can reap good financial reward for traders. The younger roots are often exported to Japan and within Vietnam; as well as being used fresh in cooking, it's processed for medicinal use or as an instant tea powder.

Na Ri district is famous for its vermicelli mien noodles. The canna root that it's made from is easy to grow and it's then sold to local manufacturers to produce and package the noodles before they're sold both in the province and further afield. Profit margins are low and cash flow causes problems for the smaller producers, but the noodles are good quality and in demand for special occasions and Tet.

Most produce, including mien, doesn't get any further than the local markets. Quantities aren't usually high enough to attract the interest of large companies further afield and transportation is difficult and expensive.

The market in Bac Kan town is certainly worth a visit in the early morning, as traders and farmers arrive ready to sell their goods.

The market sells all the goods you'll see at wet markets elsewhere, but sprawls across a large square as well as having inside areas where most of the meat stalls can be found. Be warned it's hot and smelly. But the stall holders are full of laughter and smiles for outsiders, who are very few and far between.

Bac Kan town can be reached by bus from Ba Dinh bus station, via Thai Nguyen. Once in the town a few accommodation options are available. Try Thuan Ngo Hotel next to the station, which has clean and large en suite rooms for 250,000 VND to 300,000 VND, not including breakfast. From there take local buses or try to hire a motorbike but be warned, the roads are bad and distances deceptive. Alternatively, hire a car for a day or so from Hanoi for around 2 million VND for a day trip, or more if you want to stay for a couple of days and travel around.

Thay and Tay Phuong Pagodas

If you haven't had a good mountainside pagoda experience, these two spots (with confusingly similar names) are some of the oldest and most historically important pagodas in Vietnam, reachable via an easy daytrip.

The first of the two, Chua Thay or 'Master's Pagoda', is about 19km from Hanoi. Just head southwest out of Hanoi on Duong Lang-Hoa Lac, take a right turn, go under the new flyover, and it's about 2km to the village.

The surrounding area features 16 hills jutting up from the farmland, likened to the body of a dragon jutting out from the sea. The largest hill is considered the head, and that's where the 11th century Chua Thay is located. You'll be greeted by a beautiful reflecting pond (Dragon Lake) featuring two bridges built in 1602, and a stage for water puppet shows, one of the oldest in Vietnam. At the end of the lake sits the main temple building, dedicated to a monk named Tu Dao Hanh who lived back in the 12th century. Inside three statues represent the monk in different forms.

As you're facing the temple, walk left towards the mountain to find the steps leading to the hilltop pagoda complex. It's about a 50m vertical ascent, and once you hump up, you'll find a collection of charming old buildings and shrines perched on the mountain, along with a natural cave shrine. The spot is a bit reminiscent of a mini Marble Mountain (located just to the south of Da Nang). A lot of complicated history and lore lies behind the shrines and the caves in the area, so if you really want all the info, try for a guided tour be sure to negotiate a price in advance. Even if you don't care for the history lesson, it's a pretty spot to visit.

The next stop is Tay Phuong. Head back to Duong Lanh, turn right, and take a right about 5km further on. There's no sign for the pagoda on the main road, but look out for one for Thach That, which is the district you are heading to (the village is called Yen). From there, it's 10km to the temple, and signs lead the way.

Once again, you'll have to walk up a few hundred steps to the pagoda. Tay Phuong is a national treasure thanks to the phenomenal sculpture and art on display there. Most notable are the likenesses of monks rendered in lacquered jackfruit wood dating from the Tay Son period, just before the 1800s. These are a cut above a lot of pagoda sculpture in terms of subtlety and detail and seem to be even finer than the examples of the genre on display in the Fine Arts museum in Hanoi.

In the central chamber of the pagoda, there's a striking rendering of a '1000-eyed, 1000-armed' Bodhisattva, with a scintillating brass-coloured finish (though we wish someone would dust it now and again so it'd really scintillate). Behind that is a cluster of statues, at the centre of which is a very fine, very eerie ascetic monk. In the dimly lit area, he looks as if he might come to life at any moment. Again, hire a good guide to get the complete lowdown on the art and history of the spot, but even without a guide there's plenty to see. Admission is 5,000 dong, hours 07:00 to 18:00 daily.

The road through Yen village continues on towards Son Tay, so you can combine this pagoda tour with a trip to Ba Vi, though it's a big day of sightseeing, so you might want to plan an overnight there.

Co Loa Citadel

This is the easiest of the Hanoi daytrips, about 16km outside the city.

The main draw here is that it's one of the oldest structures still extant from Vietnamese history (though Cham and Sa Huynh culture is much older).

The ancient, spiral-shaped citadel dates back to the third century BC, with a few of the ancient ramparts remaining but hard to spot among the more recent construction. There's a reflecting pond with a statue of King An Duong Vuong shooting a bow and arrow. The weapon had magical powers and he was supposed to use it to fight off Chinese invaders, but his enemy got hold of it and used it to defeat him, ushering in nearly a century of Chinese rule.

There are three sites to visit here: a small pagoda dedicated to the king's daughter (who figured prominently in the tale of woe behind the temple's history), the Am Mi Chau pagoda, which now houses a museum displaying archaeological finds from the area dating back as much as 5,000 years (though you'll find more of the same and better at the History Museum in Hanoi), and also the temple dedicated to the king himself, which has a good display of Buddhist statuary dating back several hundred years.

There's a lot of lore and history here, more so than the other sites listed in this section, so try to hire a guide in Hanoi to give you the rundown.

Admission gives access to all the sites, so keep your ticket handy.

How to get there

The Citadel can be reached by leaving Hanoi to the northeast. Take the Chuong Duong bridge over the Hong River out of town to where the road joins up with Highway 1. You'll cross another river 11km later via an old, narrow steel bridge. Take the immediate left, and follow that road as it meets Highway 3, keep straight, and after about 4km there's a sign on the left marking the turn for the site on the right. Turn off for the Citadel. It's another kilometre further down that road and well marked.

Co Loa Citadel
16km outside Hanoi
Daily 08:00 to 17:00.
Admission: 5,000 dong

Ba Vi National Park

If you're planning to visit only one national park in Vietnam, other parks, like Bach Ma near Hue, should be higher up on your list than Ba Vi.

Nevertheless, it's a beautiful park and if you just want a quiet getaway for a day or so, it's a fine choice.

The main attraction at the park is the mountain itself, which rises to more than 1,200m above sea level. There's a very good road leading 12km up to the summit. You can hike or cycle it if you like, but the rest of us mere mortals should take a car or motorbike. The road is narrow and twisty, but far from the worst we've seen on that score in Vietnam. If you're doing it on a motorbike, make sure you're an expert in negotiating first gear.

The foliage, as you ascend the mountain, is green and pristine, and the atmosphere is serene. It's worth going just for that wonderful feeling of relaxation that comes over you the higher you go. Many of the trees in the park are marked according to species, but only in Vietnamese.

Once at the top, you'll have two hikes ahead of you to mountaintop temples. Den Thuong is the easier of the two, at about 600 steps to the top. The second goes to a temple honouring of Ho Chi Minh, called Bac Ho. We tackled the first on our most recent visit. The stairs get progressively trickier near the top, once you pass the first temple, to the smaller shrine above. The views from the top are excellent, or at least, they would have been had we gone on a clear day. We went in the cool season when the mountain is generally shrouded in mist, which is way cool, but we couldn't see a thing.

Food and refreshments are available at the top of the paved road. Other hikes around the slopes of the mountain are possible if you're here for more than a day or so.

Accommodation is available at the Ba Vi Guest House (T: (034) 881 197) which has 30 rooms. Fan rooms cost 150,000 dong and air-con goes for 200,000 dong.

About 4km from the base along the summit road is accommodation and half a dozen restaurants to choose from. There are also tennis courts and a huge swimming pool, though if you think of it as a small artificial lake, you're less likely to be put off by the colour of the water. It's a ghost town in low season, October through March, but otherwise fills up on weekends and holidays in fair weather.

Some lower-key attractions lie within the national park boundary surrounding the base of the mountain: several springs, a lake, and some waterfalls, all within a few kilometres and well marked. Take a look at the map at the main entrance. There's no real set-up to receive foreign visitors, so if you're thinking of exploring the park properly, be sure to look into your options with someone knowledgeable in Hanoi before you arrive.

The closest ATMs to Ba Vi are in Son Tay town, 10km from the mountain. There's internet there, and to a lesser extent as you head towards the mountain. There's a post office in Van Hoa along DT 414 (Route 32) 5 km from the park entrance. The park's main gate is open from 05:00 to 21:00. Admission is 15,000 dong, plus a small charge for your vehicle depending on size. T: (0343) 880 010. Very little English is spoken.

How to get there

Ba Vi is located 68km from the outskirts of Hanoi, and you'll have to budget a couple of hours just to get there, due to traffic. Head out of Hanoi to the southwest crossing the To Tich bridge onto Tran Duy Hung which becomes Duong Lang-Hoa Lac just outside the city limits. From there, it's 30km to where the road ends. Take a right there, on Route 21, and proceed 26km to the village of Son Tay. There you'll take a hairpin turn on the road towards Khoang Xanh and the entrance to the mountain is 10km further along. Resist taking the more northern route that leaves Hanoi on Cau Giay in Quan Cau Giay. The road is dreadful.

If you're travelling under your own steam, when you're done with the park, there is a road around the park which is reportedly quite beautiful which leads 100km to Hoa Binh. Again, take a look at the map at the entrance to the park to get a sense of it.

By bus, depart from My Dinh station or Kim Ma (No. 201 it's a local bus so might be a bit slow) for Son Tay and flag down a local bus from there toward Khoang Xanh. Or take local bus no. 214 from My Dinh which turns down the Khoang Xanh road. Alternatively try to book a xe om from Son Tay. It should cost about 200,000 dong to take you to the summit, have your driver wait for you while you visit a temple, and return.

Performing arts

Thang Long Water Puppets

Thang Long Water Puppet Theatre is the place to go to experience a traditional Vietnamese water puppet performance.

The theatre itself is not traditional shows used to be performed in rice paddies and a few bells and whistles have been added these days, but otherwise the hour-long show is the real deal, with live traditional music thrown in as well.

Water puppetry in Vietnam is documented as far back as the establishment of Thang Long (Hanoi) as the capital of the country 1,000 years ago, although it may have existed even before this. After 1010, legend has it that the country went through a stable period, with no wars, and handicrafts were able to flourish. At the same time, festivals and ceremonies became popular, providing an opportunity for artists to perform puppet shows both on land and water.

Thang Long Water Puppet Theatre, on the northeastern bank of Hoan Kiem Lake, is certainly not 1,000 years old, nor reminiscent of the traditional environment in which water puppet shows would have taken place, but if you want to see this art form it's easy accessible, reasonably priced and an authentic performance.

The theatre is more comfortable than we remember from the first visit we made a decade ago; we're sure than in those days the seats were wooden benches, prone to sending your bum to sleep. Now the hall boasts rows of standard theatre-style, green-cushioned chairs, with a "pond" at the front instead of a stage.

The show starts with a short musical composition on traditional instruments, played by the small orchestra to the side of the pond; it's introduced in Vietnamese and English and then the puppet performances begin with a prelude by clown Teu, a funny looking puppet with sprouting hair. Then things really come to life, with a band of drummers taking to the….

Massages and spas

Where can I get a good massage in Hanoi?

Massages in Hanoi range from very cheap and cheerful foot massages through to high-end luxury spas, where you'll pay nearly $100 for just an hour of pampering. The choice can be overwhelming but here's a selection of places we think are worth checking out.

Our top pick by a long shot is over West Lake way: Yakushi. This is a no-nonsense traditional spot where the focus is on health and healing rather than frills and flowers. Yakushi is popular with expats for a reason: it's clean, friendly, well priced, and the massages are fantastic. We've tried and tested the hot stone and shiatsu massages, but also offered are Swedish, aromatherapy, acupressure with oil and lymphatic drainage. A Swedish one-hour massage costs 250,000 dong, hot stone is 270,000 dong and the rest are 290,000 dong, with clear signs asking that you do not tip staff.

If you have time and want to float rather than walk out, add in a facial, starting at 350,000 dong for 75 minutes. Book well in advance, especially for evenings and weekends. They are responsive to emails if you don't have a phone to hand. The centre is located down an alley off Xuan Dieu Street just near Saint Honore don't mistake the different spa on the main road for it.

For a cheap and cheerful foot massage, we really liked no-fuss Van Xuan, which has three locations. We tried the Ly Quoc Su outlet, and had an excellent back, shoulders, arms and foot massage for just $6. Your feet soak in blissful hot water while they massage the rest of your body using acupressure only while seated (a proper full-body massage is a different treatment done on massage tables).

We also tried a foot massage at Wonder Foot nearby on Nha Tho, and while it was pretty good and set in a pleasant upstairs room away from the ruckus below, we were a bit put off by unfriendly staff insisting that the price did not include service, that would cost an additional 70,000 dong.

Giving back

Humanitarian Services for Children of Vietnam

Humanitarian Services for Children of Vietnam (HSCV) was founded in 2002 to help orphans, homeless children and other children living in poverty in Hanoi and surrounding areas through the provision of food, shelter, clothing, health and education.

The organisation was set up by American Chuck DeVet and his daughter Annetta, following a visit to Vietnam in 2001. Their experiences drove them to want to help needy children in the country, and after further visits they decided to set up HSCV in the Hanoi area, which was less well served by charitable organisations than the south.

HSCV operates a number of programmes: educational scholarships, rice distribution, bicycle donations, wheelchair distribution, orthopaedic surgery, medical missions and orphanages.

One of HSCV's newest initiatives is a girls' foster home in Hanoi. Opened in 2011, it is now home to 14 girls between the ages of four and 18. The girls are supported at the home by a head of home, a house mother, a social worker and two assistants. They attend school, are provided with meals and receive medical care. The difference the home makes to these girls is evident: it is a nurturing environment in which they can overcome past problems with the aid of the helpers and the companionship of the other girls. The girls arrived at the home through a number of different channels, such as Blue Dragon, a foundation that supports kids in crisis in Vietnam.

A new home near the existing location was rented this year and the Hanoi International Women's Club has donated funds for the purchase of essential equipment for setting up another house for girls.

The children helped by HSCV have diverse backgrounds. Huong and one of her sisters are an example. They resorted to begging after their father deserted the family and were left in the care of their maternal grandmother. When their grandmother died they moved in with their cousin and her brother, and the four of them, all under 18, lived in a squalid one-room apartment, supported solely by the cousin's meagre income. Huong now lives at the girls' foster home, is an excellent student and helps the other girls with their studies and daily life; although she's always wanted to be a singer, she now wants to become a social worker to help vulnerable girls like herself. Her youngest sister, aged five, has also now moved into the foster home.

Mai grew up in Dien Bien province. Her father earnt a small living as a carpenter but her mother was unable to work due to a heart condition. When Mai was three she fell into her father's saw and severed her right arm above the elbow. Despite this, she learnt to ride a bike, wash clothes, cook, sew and knit. Later, both of her parents were imprisoned for drug-related incidents and her father died while in prison. While her mother was in prison in Hanoi, Mai applied for an educational scholarship from HSCV and studied at the Special Education Division at the Hanoi Teacher Training University. She has now graduated and plans to return to her hometown to work as a teacher.

The money donated by Travelfish.org US$100 will be used to purchase sewing equipment for the girls' foster homes such as scissors, braid, thread and material. To both entertain the girls during the school holidays and provide them with skills, a sewing machine has been purchased for the new home and a sewing programme will be set up by a member of HIWC.

The HSCV website provides more information on the foster home and other programmes. It also makes it easy to donate! Each program provides a breakdown of funds needed for its operation so, for example, you can choose to donate a bicycle, sponsor a child in education, pay the rent on the foster home or just donate a fixed sum.

Each month a Travelfish.org writer selects a charity or non-government organisation that they believe does excellent work on their patch in Southeast Asia. They write about them and we donate $100, a small way for us to give something back to the region. If you're looking to give back too, please consider giving a little cash as well.

Interesting buildings

Heritage house at 87 Ma May St

Dating back to the 19th century, this special house is a great example of the type of architecture that once prevailed throughout Hanoi's busy Old Quarter.

It might be hard to imagine, but Ma May Street was once located on the banks of the Red River, in the midst of a commercial harbour. The mainly wooden house at 87 Ma May was built at the end of the 19th century, when Vietnam was under French rule, as a shop and residence. It was similar to many others in the area built and used by shopkeepers that were later pulled down and rebuilt into more modern styles. Various families lived at number 87 until 1999, when the house was the first to be restored back to its original state in the Old Quarter. It was renovated again in 2013.

The narrow frontage is typical of the traditional houses from this period, with buildings and courtyards stretching back behind allowing light and air to flow through an otherwise dark space.

The shop was located at the front, with a courtyard to its rear and then another building behind containing the living area. Behind this is another courtyard and then a kitchen and bathroom are located to the rear. Upstairs is the bedroom and ancestor altar.

The house is an excellent glimpse into Hanoi's rapidly vanishing architectural heritage. The downstairs shop space is given over to, well, a shop selling good quality lacquerware, but the rest of the house is set up as it would have been back in the day, with antique furniture and other old......

Hanoi Opera House

The Hanoi Opera House, located in the French Quarter, is an attraction in itself. Do try to catch a show here so you can experience the building in all its majesty.

The neo-classically styled Opera House was built over the decade running from 1901, and the official site says 300 workers were on the site daily, using 35,000 bamboo poles and concrete blocks in its construction we're not sure of the breakdown between the poles and blocks? The steps cascading down to the square in front were designed for ostentatious drop offs and pick ups by the cars of colonial officials; these days you can call a Grab bike or taxi to collect you. It's not quite the same in terms of being salubrious, but it's certainly convenient.

The design is said to have been inspired by ancient Greek architecture and the neo-Baroque style of Charles Garnier, who designed the elaborate Paris Opera (or Palais Garnier), opened in 1875. Once opened, the Hanoi Opera House during the colonial era was used by touring foreign artists, usually performing French and Italian operas for mostly French opera-goers and wealthy Vietnamese, four times a week.

After the ejection of the French, the Opera House became the site of more political activities, with the first National Assembly of the Democratic Republic of Vietnam held here in 1945. Later, the building returned to its original purpose, with Vietnamese operas and musicals being staged here, some with Soviet assistance.

The building underwent a renovation in 1997; the interior in particular is lavish and characterful. These days Western operas are occasionally mounted, and there are also performances by visiting classical orchestras, and a whole gamut of entertainments, such as puppet shows, ballets and nights of traditional Vietnamese song and drama.

Historic attractions
Ho Chi Minh's Mausoleum
In that great communist tradition, the liberator of Vietnam Ho Chi Minh remains lying in state so his admirers can pay their respects, even nearly five decades after his death.

The mausoleum is set in sprawling Ba Dinh Square, where Ho Chi Minh read out the Declaration of Independence in 1945. This is easily Hanoi's most popular attraction, at least when it comes to something you need to queue for. We showed up just after gates opened to find a line already snaking for hundreds of metres outside the entrance gate. Entrance is free, and your bags will need to be X-rayed, but you can keep them with you. We waited for around 40 minutes to eventually enter the small room where his embalmed body rests under subdued lights. Visitors circumnavigate the glass sarcophagus holding Bac Ho, in literally guarded silence, for about 60 seconds.

Considering how long he's been lying here, Vietnam's founding father is looking pretty good a bit like he's just taking a nap. Teams of experts from Russia still visit regularly to consult and help out with his preservation.

While the room is small, the austere mausoleum itself is huge. Built between 1973 and 1975 with Soviet assistance and modelled after the one in Moscow where Lenin is on display, it's more brutalist in style than anything else and the approach, particularly given how slow it is, is all rather dramatic.

You can keep your phones and camera gear with you, but photography is strictly not permitted. While people were taking photos of the gardens and exterior of the mausoleum as we waited, nobody dared try anything under the watchful eye of the guards

Presidential Palace and Ho Chi Minh's House on Stilts
A visit to the exterior of the Presidential Palace, plus a house Ho Chi Minh lived in from 1954 to 1958, then his so-called House on Stilts, and

his car collection, naturally follows a stop at nearby Ho Chi Minh's Mausoleum.

Simply follow the crowds when you leave the mausoleum and you'll find yourself at the ticket booth to here, with the first stop in this complex being the exterior of the ochre-coloured Presidential Palace.

Today the palace is the official home of Vietnam's president, but it was originally the residence of the French Governor-General of Indochina. The ornate 30-room palace, built in Beaux Arts style at the start of the 20th century by French architect Auguste Henri Vildieu, is also used occasionally by the government for state receptions, particularly when heads of state visit. Architectural Digest named the palace one of the 13 most beautiful in the world in 2016.

For obvious symbolic reasons, Ho Chi Minh refused to move into the palace when the French were ousted in 1954, though he did receive guests there. Instead he moved into a modest cottage on the grounds while he waited for a house on stilts he commissioned to be built

You'll file past the several rooms of the first house, kept absolutely pristine, and a garage where his collection of well-preserved, gleaming cars remain stored behind

Chuong Duong Bridge

The Chuong Duong Bridge opened in 1985, and is one of the main bridges that moves traffic across the Red River in Hanoi.

The four-lane, steel span bridge's claim to fame is that it was the first sizeable bridge designed and built by Vietnamese workers, with no international assistance. Located just south of Long Bien Bridge, and beginning near the Old Quarter, it took almost two years to complete. Unlike Long Bien, which is worth checking out in person, you wouldn't come out of your way to see heavily trafficked Chuong Duong, but knowing its name and position will help orientate yourself in the city. In 2014 it was estimated that about 20,000 cars and 210,000 motorbikes crossed the bridge daily.

Thang Long Citadel

The sprawling grounds of the World Heritage-listed Thang Long Citadel are a palimpsest across which Hanoi's history has been written and re-written. You can easily spend a few hours here exploring the grounds and the archaeological dig just across the road.

The citadel site has been a continuous seat of power for some 1,300 years. It most recently operated as a military base until it was opened to the public to mark the 1,000-year anniversary of Hanoi and its UNESCO World Heritage listing. Despite being sandwiched between four busy roads, the complex feels like an escape from the city. There are two sub-sections: the citadel grounds and buildings, plus the dig at 18 Hoang Dieu Street across the road.

The site was first used as the Dai Lai Citadel when the area, then known as Giao Chau, was under Chinese rule from the seventh to ninth centuries; foundations of wooden buildings, tools, furniture, wells and drainage ditches from this period have been found at the dig.

When the Ly Dynasty (1009-1225) shifted the capital of its empire from Hoa Lu to the Dai Lai Citadel, changing its name to Thang Long in 1010. They built a new citadel comprising a Forbidden City home to the Emperor's Palace nested within two sets of walls. The area within the outer walls was known as Kinh Thanh (Imperial City), and the space within the second set of walls was Hoang Thanh, or the Imperial Citadel. The citadel remained here through dynasties over the next centuries, with additions including palaces, pavilions, towers, pagodas, temples and shrines.

In 1805, when the capital was relocated to Hue, King Gia Long demolished the citadel and replaced it with one in French Vauban style, which he used when he travelled in the north, though he kept the Kinh Thanh Palace; it was pulled down in 1815 as its wooden columns had rotted. In 1897, the French demolished the citadel completely to make way for a modern quarter as they planned to build a new city. After 1954, the area became the head office of the ministry of defence and the commander-in-chief of the Vietnamese People's Army

Long Bien Bridge

Impressive Long Bien Bridge, which spans Hanoi's Red River to connect Hoan Kiem and Long Bien districts, was built by the French colonists at the turn of the 20th century.

Considered one of the most stunning bridges in the world when it opened in 1903, the cantilever bridge originally had 19 spans and was designed by Gustav Eiffel, the engineer best known for his eponymous landmark in Paris. The approximately 2.5-kilometre (some say 1.7-kilometre) bridge, built by thousands of Vietnamese workers, was first known as Doumer Bridge, after the French governor-general Paul Doumer, who was responsible for setting up the French administration and implementing huge public works projects. Ironically perhaps, the Vietnamese say the bridge allowed for the easy transport of rice to Dien Bien Phu, helping them win independence against the French there in their battle of 1954. The last contingent of French soldiers retreated across the bridge on 9 October 1954, after withdrawing from the Citadel; a day later victory over the French was declared. The bridge was then renamed Long Bien.

The majestic old bridge, its ironwork now slowly and evocatively rusting and making for some great photos, suffered at the hands of war over the years, thanks to its strategic location it was once the only bridge that connected Hanoi to the port of Haiphong. It was bombed by the Americans in 1966-7 and 1972, eviscerating seven of the original spans; the latter attack caused it to shut for a year. In 1983, the nearby Chuong Duong Bridge opened, and this became the main thoroughfare for traffic to the north, though since then four other bridges have also opened as the city has boomed. As of 2015, only $150,000 was reportedly being spent annually on around 80 workers to scrape rust, repaint, clean and replace sleepers

Front Guide
Surviving Hanoi traffic on foot

Hanoi is one of the craziest places in Southeast Asia to roam the streets, whether on some form of transport or on foot. Here's how to get out alive.

It starts from the minute you leave the airport or station. I recall arriving back here in 2010, early one morning after a train from Hue, and literally closing my eyes as the driver shot across crossroads, and through red lights, at speed. And if you're coming from the airport, you have the terrors of the highway to face. I have to say, that feeling doesn't go away altogether, but you learn to cope with it.

But given most visitors to Hanoi are either a passenger in which case you need to adopt the deep breaths, close your eyes and prayer approach or walking, here are a few tips for surviving the traffic when walking in Hanoi. Remember, walking is still the cheapest way to get around you can do it! (Though some argue you're best to take a motorbike and spend your walking time chilling.)

The main tricks to learn are about crossing the road. Anyone who's been here will already know the "rules": walk slowly but steadily across the road, allowing vehicles to move around you and don't stop suddenly except in an emergency. This works, but you still need to be alert don't expect all the drivers to be fully concentrating, especially in these days of mobile phones, and expect traffic to come from all angles, even on a one-way street. So keep looking around as you're walking, just in case.

Also bear in mind that while Old Quarter is particularly hectic, at least the traffic tends to move slowly, and it's mainly bikes. Once you get out of Old Quarter and onto some of the main roads, you'll be faced with a lot more cars as well as buses and trucks. Adopt the same approach but be even more aware and take your time to choose a good moment to cross there will be occasional breaks in the traffic so be patient. Sometimes you'll find so-called pedestrian crossings at traffic lights, but still take care when crossing and bear in mind that traffic turning right doesn't tend to stop at a red light; so even if the little man is green, there might be traffic passing by.

If you're with a group, line up and cross together, giving traffic more room to manoeuvre around you. Do not just wander across in a loosely formed clump or in single file.

Unfortunately, it's not just when *crossing* the road that you'll need to watch for traffic. Footpaths are frequently non-existent, especially in built-up, heavily populated areas with narrow streets, such as Old Quarter. This means you will often have to walk in the road. I was always taught that you should walk facing oncoming traffic, and that rule applies here. Well, as far as it can, given traffic doesn't necessarily drive on the right side of the road or the right way down a one-way street. But it's a place to start. Single file is best, unless the road's really quiet, otherwise you'll end up constantly having to move out of the way of traffic.

Also bear in mind that traffic sometimes drives on the footpath, particularly when trying to avoid traffic jams on main roads. You could do as my friend does and refuse to move out of the way while giving the driver a "this is my space, get back on the road you idiot" stare, or you could just move out of the way. I'd suggest the latter.

A final word of warning: do not become complacent. Yes, traffic will move around you but don't treat the roads as the footpath even if drivers treat the footpaths like the roads.

The Essentials

While the city is developing a bit of a sprawl, Hanoi's centre can be split into three main areas, all of which are within walking distance of one another.

The Old Quarter remains the most popular, interesting and inexpensive part of Hanoi to stay in. Wedged to the north of Hoan Kiem Lake, the area is characterised by a twisting mess of narrow roads and alleys, lots of attractive old buildings, interesting street scenes and plenty of noise.

The Old Quarter (or Pho Co, old streets) is home to streets named after the goods that were traditionally sold on them. The names usually start with hang, which means "something you sell", and then the thing itself. Some of these names may date back as far as 800 years, when trade guilds formed to market the goods they produced in outlying craft villages. Back then, the streets were just lines of makeshift stalls. When they eventually built on the land, they went deep and high because they were taxed by width of frontage that's the explanation for all those skinny buildings, with a shop kept upfront. Each guild also poured some profits into the building of temples at which to pray for prosperity, and you can still find several along some streets. The most famous and best to visit is Bach Ma Temple along Hang Buom.

Many of the streets have changed with the times, especially in the southern part of the Old Quarter, which has been given over to tourism and its allied businesses. But a surprising number of streets still sell what they were named for centuries ago, and yet more have found new specialties that make them worth seeking out.

While the names of Hanoi's classic streets are colourful, unfortunately, they sometimes change every few blocks Bat Dan, Hang Bo, Hang Bac and Hang Mam are all the same exact street. This makes it tricky to get around, since you can be headed straight to your hotel and not even know it.

To the south of the lake is the French Quarter, home to Central Hanoi's poshest hotels: the Sofitel Legend Metropole and the Hilton Hanoi Opera, as well as the Opera House itself. Here you'll also find some of Hanoi's ritziest restaurants the Club Opera and the Press Club, as the well as the Museum of History and the Revolution Museum. It's a good place for a visit even if you're not staying here it's much better laid-out, with broad, tree-lined boulevards and, compared to the rest of Hanoi, moderate street traffic. Come evening, the streets are relatively deserted.

The western part of the city is home to West Lake, the Citadel, the Ho Chi Minh Mausoleum Complex and a bunch of museums. Those visiting the attractions will often find themselves in this part of town, though there are not many hotels. When visiting West Lake in summer, be sure to look out for the lotus-flower farms rimming the lake an excellent photo op.

A word about the traffic. It's not uncommon to see foreigners standing on the curb, frozen in fear, waiting for a break in the onslaught of bikes, cyclos, trucks, vendor carts, and motorbikes (with two tons of bagged cement balancing, unfastened, on the back) ... but the break never comes. The terrifying solution is that you must simply step right into the street. Be sure to look carefully for vehicles moving in the wrong direction first, and give approaching vehicles room to manoeuvre around you without smashing into something or someone. What you'll find is that the traffic simply flows around you as you proceed slowly and steadily forward. Stop, while crossing, if you must, but stand firm and do not back up! That's the surest way to flummox the flow. Stand there like a pylon until the way forward is clear. And, again, keep an eye out for traffic going the wrong way.

Where should I stay in Hanoi?
By far the bulk of tourists and travellers opt for lodgings in the Old Quarter, which has the best selection of accommodation, from budget guesthouses through to comfortable midrange hotels, and even luxury hotels are popping up along the old streets. The French Quarter and West Lake have the bulk of plush hotels.

Picking a hotel in Hanoi can be daunting. Good hotels go bad, and bad hotels become good at a rate that even the most diligent travel researcher is hard-pressed to keep up with. Many travellers prefer to book ahead in Hanoi, and we can't blame them cheap digs fill up quickly during peak times and the last thing you want to do, especially after getting off an international flight, is hump from place to place. But committing to one hotel, sight unseen, is risky. Book one or two days, so if you don't like what you get, you can easily switch venues. And if you're happy where you are, rarely do hotels refuse when guests wish to extend their stay.

Sights and attractions

Hanoi has some fine spots to visit, but really, the attraction of Hanoi is the very town itself. Travellers who arrive in Vietnam via Hanoi are usually too busy taking it all in to worry about touring the sights. And those who wind up their trip here are usually toured out and just want to relax. Both groups end up wandering around the Old Quarter, eating and drinking, and revelling in the beauty and madness of the city. A third group pre-books a sightseeing tour, takes in all the culture, but maybe misses out on the city itself. If you really want to do both, you should dedicate at least a week to Hanoi alone. But if you have to choose, we see no downside to blowing off the tourist attractions and just immersing yourself in one of the great cities of Southeast Asia.

Maps

Numerous maps of Hanoi are available at magazine kiosks and bookstores throughout the city, as well as from roving booksellers, and start at about 20,000 VND.

The "Vietnam Tourist Map" by the Nhat Xuat Ban Ban Do company features a map of the whole country on one side with a bare sketch of the road network. On the reverse, the map of Hanoi is good for one-way streets, but the Old Quarter is small and hard to read, and there's no street index. There's also a map of Saigon.

The same company also publishes "Du Lich Hanoi Tourist Map" with Northern Vietnam on one side (and better coverage of roads) and a blow up of their Hanoi map on the other side, with one-way streets indicated, and a pretty good street index.

In general, for the Old Quarter, you may do just as well picking up a free map from your hotel many of them are good enough.

The freebie "Map of Hanoi City" provided by the Tourist Information Centre and available at most hotels and travel agencies will do at a pinch, but it's packed with ads, lacks detail, the street index is small and one-way streets are not indicated.

Hanoi is an ideal place to stock up on reading material and maps for the rest of your trip too. The wandering book sellers are sure to approach you with their stacks, all of which can be bought a bit more cheaply at a proper book store, but you can usually bargain the price down to a reasonable mark-up. If you want to check out a merchant with walls, try:

Bookworm 44 Chau Long, Hanoi. T: (04) 3715 3711. bookworm@fpt.vn. Hours: 09:00 to 19:00.

Trang Tien Bookstore 44 Trang Tien, Hanoi. T: (04) 826 2934, F: (04) 934 1591. Hours: 08:00 to 21:00.

Secondhand books and book exchanges are available at some of the backpacker orientated hotels as well as at a few travel agents:

Love Planet 25 Hang Bac, Hanoi: 1 Hang Buom, Hanoi. T: (04) 6683 5539, loveplanet@hn.vnn.vn.

Communications

The international code for Vietnam is 84, and the city code for Hanoi is 04. Many cell phone numbers start with 09 and in some cases 01. When calling from oversees, drop the zero before the city code and cell phone numbers. Dial-out codes differ from country to country . If you plan to make calls from your room, look for hotels that offer IDD (International Direct Dialling). But this is very expensive far better to drag yourself to a cyber-cafe that offers internet phone services.

Internet

If you're got a WiFi enabled PDA or laptop you'll never be far from a signal in Hanoi as most hotels and cafes offer free WiFi, often without even requiring a password. Many hotels also have internet stations in reception for guest use and more than a few places supply desktop computers in their deluxe rooms. Failing that, internet cafes are rarely more than 10,000 VND per hour though you may need to vie with the local kids for a station. Once place at 82 Ma May also offers international calls, CD burning and SIM cards.

Hanoi newspapers

If you're looking to keep up-to-date on the latest grain prices and other economic gems, Vietnam News is for you. Otherwise keep an eye out for imported dailies, like the International Herald Tribune.

Emergencies

Hospitals

Hanoi has adequate hospitals, though for serious injuries, evacuation to Bangkok is a good idea make sure you have travel insurance. Hospitals in Hanoi include:

International SOS 51 Xuan Dieu, Hanoi. T: (04) 3934 0666, F: (04) 3934 0556. 24-hour emergency.

Hanoi Family Medical Practice Van Phuc Compound, 298 Kim Ma, Hanoi. T: (04) 843 0748, F: (04) 846 1750. 24-hour

Medications and contraband

If you need to carry a large supply of medications into Vietnam through Hanoi, make sure they are well marked and, if possible, unopened. The authorities are very wary of drug trafficking and may, in some circumstances, suspect the worst. That said, once you're in Vietnam, many of the prescription drugs you buy back home are available over the counter at greatly reduced prices. Also, be warned that literature or visual media that might be deemed offensive (morally or politically) might be confiscated, at a minimum.

Police

When it comes to violent crime, Hanoi, in general, is remarkably safe, particularly for foreigners. This is partly because crimes against foreigners are treated more severely by the government, which wants to encourage tourism. Petty crime is also infrequent, but foreigners are sometimes the target. We've heard of cat burglaries, bag-snatching, and pockets being picked. Advice is to take out only what you need, particularly in the evening; leave the credit cards, camera and iPod behind. Other than that, the overwhelming way foreigners are robbed in Hanoi is by being overcharged. If that starts getting under your skin, read some of the crime reports from Thailand or Cambodia.

One great thing about the cops in Vietnam is that they don't hassle tourists ever. There's apparently a new policy by the government stating that if a police officer tries to extort a foreigner for money (the way they do in Laos all the time), once you report it, they will be fired immediately. This has created a relaxed climate for expats and travellers that is second-to-none in Southeast Asia. Two notable exceptions, though: helmets are mandatory for drivers AND passengers everywhere in Hanoi, and radar speed traps are increasingly common on the main arteries.

The police can however be a little slow off the block when it comes to petty crime. This can be frustrating, but it won't help to scream and stomp your feet and threaten to call your embassy. Be patient and polite at all times. All they are really going to do is fill out a report which you'll need to claim the loss on your insurance. This situation changes dramatically however if the crime is serious, especially if you have concrete information about the perpetrator. Then, they snap into action.

The emergency telephone number for the police is 113.

Common needs in Hanoi

Banks

ATMs are everywhere, especially in the Old Quarter. Almost all of them take foreign cards, but you can look for HSBC, Sacom, BIDV, ANZ and Vietcom. They all, of course, have numerous bank branches with a wide range of services and many are open on Saturday.

Although foreign exchange is available at most banks, you may end up paying US$2 to change a US$20 note. ANZ for example, charges 1% on cash transfers, with a minimum of US$2. It's double that for travellers cheques. Most hotels will change USD into VND but check their exchange rate first and compare with xe.com. Another thing to watch out for is being left with VND at the end of your trip banks are reluctant to change back into USD, due to low supply, and recent clampdowns have meant even the gold shops aren't a guaranteed source anymore.

Post offices

Hanoi GPO is located at 75 Dinh Tien Hoang, Hanoi. It's on the southeast edge of Hoan Kiem Lake, just south of Ngoc Son Pagoda and across the street you can't miss it.

T: (04) 3825 5948.

Open 07:30-18:00 Monday to Saturday, 08:00-18:00 Sunday, 09:00-18:00 public holidays.

Long distance phone services are available.

Basic postal services are also available everywhere you see the words "Buu Dien" and many hotels will handle postal services for you.

International GPO is at 6 Dinh Le, Hanoi. T: (04) 3825 4503. Open 07:30 to 18:00 Monday to Friday, 09:00 to 18:00 Saturdays, Sundays and public holidays.

If you're sending a package or letter internationally, the small office on the corner of Dinh Tien Hoang and Dinh Le, just a few doors down from the main Post Office, is a better option.

Tours

We wish we could give you an authoritative guide to the shifting sands of Hanoi travel agencies, but such is beyond the capabilities of any mere mortal. So many factors come into play when booking a tour or ticket. How much are you willing to pay? What will you put up with to pay less? How many others are signed up for a tour on a given day? New agencies pop up all the time, old agencies close down. Good agencies sometimes cut corners, crappy agencies sometimes give you the time of your life.

If you're headed to Ha Long, check out our Ha Long Bay section for a series of stories on picking the right tour. Otherwise, the key destinations are sites near Ninh Binh and Sapa, though city tours, trips to the Perfume Pagoda, and tours of nearby craft villages are also available.

Our general advice is, shop around for the best price, but be warned: the best price is not always the best trip for you. Nail down specifics: mode of transport, class of accommodation, number of people on the tour, available activities. As a rule of thumb, any ticket seller who wavers on answering or is obviously making things up as they go, is a red flag. But here's the kicker: the tour they are lying about may actually be fine, they just don't know one way or the other! You see our dilemma.

There are also plenty of tours to Vietnam offered by international adventure tour companies that include Hanoi as a part of a larger tour.

Finally, you will find a Tourist Information Centre smack on the northern shore of Hoan Kiem Lake (on 7 Dinh Tien Hoang south of Cau Go). They tout tours by AsianaTravelMate, and unless they are giving you ingots of gold as a parting gift, much better deals are available elsewhere, even for a luxury tour. There is another Asiana Travel Mate at 21 Luong NgocQuyen.

Air tickets

With four providers offering domestic flights, as well as numerous international flight operators, booking in advance online is usually the cheapest and easiest option. But if you prefer to leave your plans more flexible you're unlikely to have any problems booking when you're in Vietnam, either through a travel agent or direct with the airline, as availability is good except during Christmas and the Tet holidays.

Spending in Hanoi?

While Vietnam is still a cheap place to visit, relative to costs outside of the region, inflation has recently been the highest in Asia: it peaked at more than 22 percent year on year in 2011 and clocked in at 14 percent in March 2012. The dong has also devalued. Unfortunately this means that you can't expect the bargains and cheap eats that were one of the main attractions of the country for many visitors and expats for that matter.

Let me bring this to life a little. When we first arrived in Hanoi, more than two years ago, *bun cha* was 15,000 VND. That meant that at our local *bun cha* stall we could get lunch and a beer for 27,000 VND under a pound. *Bun cha* is now 25,000 VND minimum more often around the 35,000 VND mark. That's a 66 percent price rise; expect similar increases for other street food.

Food in restaurants is difficult to give an average price for. If you go to one of the tourist-orientated food places in Old Quarter, such as Gecko, Provecho or Le Pub, expect to pay around 80,000 to 120,000 VND for a burger or chilli or something in that vein, more if you want pizza. Restaurants that specialise in Vietnamese, such as New Day or Ladybird, have some cheaper options, but by the time you've ordered a bit of this and a bit of that, it can come in at a similar price. Of course, you can spend a lot more if you want to.

As for beer, well the place we used to eat *bun cha* was particularly cheap, at 12,000 VND, but bia Hanoi seems relatively unaffected by inflation: it's still easy enough to find for about 15,000 VND a bottle on the street. *Bia hoi*, on the other hand, increases every year. Yes, it's still cheap, but at *bia hoi* international corner it's now 6,000 VND, whereas it was 3,000 VND when we travelled here in 2009. Elsewhere prices are around 5,000 to 7,000 VND, more for *bia tuoi* (the posher *bia hoi*). Prices of other beers in bars and restaurants vary quite notably: as a guide, a small draft Tiger is around 30,000 VND and a large one 50,000 VND. Local beers are a bit cheaper.

It's now difficult to get a room in Hanoi for under US$10 a night expect to pay US$15 minimum for a basic room, $25 for something a bit more spacious and well-equipped and $40+ for a midrange place. Dorm beds are US$6 and so remain the cheapest option

Finally, transport has really taken a hit. Taxis and xe oms charge more because fuel prices have increased so much, and train and plane fares are also notably higher than they were a couple of years ago. As an indication: large taxis are around 13,000 VND per kilometre, a taxi from the airport to Hanoi is 315,000 VND, xe oms charge as much as they can get away with (but you should aim for under 10,000 VND per kilometre), a one-way flight to Danang is around 1.5 million, and the soft sleeper train to Hue is 850,000 VND (more through an agent).

So where does that leave you in terms of overall budget for your holiday in Hanoi? If you are happy to sleep in a dorm bed, live off street food and a few *bia hoi* each day, walk everywhere, maybe visit a museum every now and again, and don't do any shopping, then you can still live on under 300,000 VND (US$15) a day excluding transport outside of Hanoi. But once you start building in Western restaurants, more alcohol, coffees, treats, shopping, better accommodation, taxis and so on, you won't be surprised to hear that the sky's the limit especially if the Sofitel Metropole Legend is more to your taste.

Getting a local SIM card in Hanoi

It's really cheap and easy to get a Vietnamese SIM card when you get to Hanoi, and if you're in the country for a while it's probably worthwhile, particularly if you plan to book hotels in advance.

I was fortunate enough to inherit a Mobifone card from some girls we were travelling with in 2009 and, surprisingly, it still worked when we got back here in 2010. My boyfriend and various visitors have all bought cards here themselves, however, with no problems

So, you need to look out for stalls advertising 'SIM The' in my experience there's never one there when you want one i.e. when you run out of credit, but keep your eyes peeled and you'll spot them around. There's a small stall on Hang Bac in the centre of Old Quarter anyway, so try there if you're having trouble. They speak some English and the last card I bought there had a sticker attached with details about the credit on the card e.g. how many international minutes it included.

Even if you don't go there, don't worry about the language barrier, particularly if you're in a touristy area, as it should be easy enough to indicate what you're after. To start with, they'll probably just sell cards and top-ups anyway, and besides they'll be in a glass case, so you can just point and wave your phone about.

If you're just on holiday then it doesn't really matter what network you're on but each time we've bought a new SIM we've been offered Vinaphone so chances are that's what you'll get. The card will probably cost 100,000VND (about $5) and that should have a little bit of credit on it but if you expect to use it a lot you might want to get one with more credit on it, or buy a top-up there and then. You can check the credit by keying *101# and OK / Call so if they're pushing you to buy extra credit you might want to do this first. Top-ups are available in a range of denominations and instructions are on the back.

A couple of final things worth noting. Firstly, you won't be able to use the card outside of the country and secondly, check you can use your phone with other SIM cards. If you're on a pay monthly deal back home you might find that your phone is locked, meaning you can't put another SIM card in. Check with your provider well before you leave home or be prepared to buy a cheap phone when you get here.

Weather & climate

How cold does it really get in Hanoi?
With the temperature dropping notably over the last week and my friend calling me this morning to ask where she could buy a heater, I thought it was an appropriate time to comment on the frequently asked question: "How cold does it get in Hanoi? ".

We arrived in Hanoi at the end of January 2010 and it was dull and grey: not the warmest welcome Hanoi could offer us. That said, it was a mild winter by all accounts I invested in a jumper, after being jumper-free for seven months of travelling, and it was a bit chilly when sitting outside drinking *bia hoi*, but nothing to moan about.

Winter 2011 however was a different story. When people in the UK heard that it was 12 degress Celsius, maybe even 10 degrees, they scoffed at my complaints of the cold. But let me tell you, 10 degrees Celsius in Hanoi is really cold.

Why? Firstly, it's damp cold: the sort of cold that feels like it's seeping under your skin and into your bones. Secondly, there's quite a wind factor, particularly if you travel by motorbike. Thirdly, there is nowhere to get warm: central heating does not exist and the buildings are not insulated.

I was cycling yes, exerting effort in an attempt to keep warm to work wearing a jacket and gloves, which I then kept on during class. And I don't work in a hut. Our apartment had constant condensation on the windows and there was no point putting on the reverse cycle air-con as the heat would just seep out through the walls and under the door. And I didn't *live* in a hut either.

So what does this mean for your winter-time visit to Hanoi? It doesn't mean don't come: I may have painted a somewhat miserable picture of the weather in the middle of winter but there's little rain, skies are blue, and a few days here in winter can be just as pleasant as at any other time of year.

The definition of winter is not always clear-cut and, as elsewhere, the weather changes throughout the season. The weather forecast at the time of writing this (December 4) is 20 degrees, and it's a beautiful day: it's cool but certainly not cold, although I expect it to be chilly enough for a jumper this evening. February is likely to be the coldest month.

Do check the weather forecast before you come, but remember, it will feel colder than the temperatures suggest.

Finally, pack appropriately. While I can't predict what this winter will be like, in late November/December a jumper or jacket and long trousers (if you get cold easily) should be sufficient, or if you're coming January through to March bring a coat and some layers. It's easy enough to buy scarves and gloves here so no need to bring them if you want to play it by ear, but it's not so easy to buy warm clothes or shoes in Western sizes, so bring those with you.

If you're planning on renting a motorbike then pack an extra layer and some gloves, and you might want to buy a face mask (as well as a helmet) when you get here while the masks are not the best health protectors, they do a good job of keeping your face warm.

And don't forget that north of Hanoi, particularly in the mountainous areas such as Sapa, will be a good deal colder.

When's the best time to visit Hanoi?

Don't be fooled by the fact Hanoi is in Southeast Asia and think shorts and T-shirts are good to go all year round. Hanoi has four seasons, and as the city's in the northern hemisphere, that means the chilly winter starts in December and steaming summer hovers around July and August. It's impossible to give firm predictions of the Hanoi weather each month, or even each season, as temperatures, rainfall and sunshine can change from day to day and often do. But we can offer some general suggestions.

Let's start with the coldest time of year. Temperatures from December to around February can drop to a cold (yes, really, it is cold) 10 degrees Celsius and reach an almost balmy 20 degrees Celsius. Ten degrees in Hanoi is a lot colder than you might expect: the humidity, wind chill factor and lack of building insulation and heating can make it feel much chillier. But that doesn't mean it's necessarily a bad time to come, as humidity is lower than at other times of year, rainfall is lower and skies are often bright blue plus you might hit a 20-degree day, and that's a great temperature for exploring the sights of the city on foot. It's also Tet time, a pretty and quiet time of year to be in the city (though do bear these points in mind).

And if it *is* cold, don't despair: all that sightseeing will keep you warm, numerous museums are worth a visit, and, if you've had enough of all that, the cold gives you an excuse to huddle up with a coffee and a good book somewhere.

April and May are generally great months to be in Hanoi weatherwise. The temperatures are consistently above 20 degrees Celsius but it's not yet reached the roasting temperatures of full-on summer. Skies are often clear and rainfall is starting to increase but is intermittent. Bear in mind though that whereas often rain in Asia is characterised as a short but heavy downpour, rain in Hanoi is often drizzle, so be prepared for grey days and bring an umbrella. That's rare though and generally this is the time of year when you can sit in a cafe with a view enjoying a coffee or beer without dripping with sweat.

After that it gets hot. June, July and August are the hottest months, with temperatures known to reach 40 degrees Celsius, though the average temperature is in the early 30s. That's still plenty hot enough, especially when combined with the high humidity. At this time of year, it's hotter than in the south of the country, where temperatures remain far more stable than in Hanoi. The heat makes doing anything a chore; as soon as you step out of the air-con you'll want to get back into the shower. So you just have to accept the sweat, grab a big bottle of water and go for it. Or give up on the exploring and plan a swimming pool visit into your day.

It's also officially rainy season, and that means regular downpours. These can last anything from 30 minutes up and usually occur at the most inconvenient times whenever that is. Carry a raincoat with you although if you get stuck, enterprising stallholders tend to whip out their raincoat rack as soon as the sky turns grey. Note that taxis can be hard to come by when it rains. Walking isn't much fun in a torrential downpour, particularly as many of the streets in Hanoi are prone to flooding. But that's another excuse to sit and do nothing but eat and drink for a while.

Temperatures drop slightly in September, but it's October we pray for, when the temperatures start to decrease and it becomes bearable to set foot outside again. October and November are similar to March and April in terms of both temperature and rainfall, although we were caught out last year with a particularly chilly and damp spell at the end of November, when the year before it was roasting.

A couple of final notes. The weather forecast that you check online is not always accurate: for example, the BBC forecast has shown it's been raining in Hanoi for the past two weeks. It hasn't. Even if the forecast shows a thunderstorm (and it's accurate!), it's not likely to last long, or will occur overnight. Storms can be cool to watch if you get a good vantage point (we suggest overlooking a lake).

Also, Hanoi is still prone to the tail edge of typhoons that race through the Gulf. At the end of June this year we had two solid days of heavy rain because of this it's unpredictable and there's very little you can do when it rains that hard for that long. It's unusual, but don't say I didn't warn you!

In summary: there really is no *bad* time to visit Hanoi. Be warned that the cold months can be a bit depressing, and if you hate the heat, don't come in June through to August. Other than that, pack and plan appropriately and don't let the weather spoil your visit.

The End

www.ingramcontent.com/pod-product-compliance
Lightning Source LLC
Chambersburg PA
CBHW031108080526
44587CB00011B/874